LIVING IN A GLASS HOUSE

RAFAELA MCEACHIN

LIVING
IN A
GLASS
HOUSE

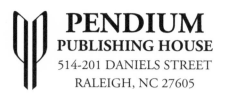

PENDIUM
PUBLISHING HOUSE
514-201 DANIELS STREET
RALEIGH, NC 27605

For information, please visit our Web site at
www.pendiumpublishing.com

PENDIUM Publishing and its logo
are registered trademarks.

LIVING IN A GLASS HOUSE
by Rafaela McEachin

ISBN: 978-1-944348-63-2

PUBLISHER'S NOTE

This book is printed on acid-free paper.

CONTENTS

Acknowledgments

First and foremost I would like to thank "God" for He is my provider, my keeper and confidence. Jesus is the reason for the season!! I would like to thank all of my family and friends for the continued support. Thank you "LisaMaria Harris" (editor) for all your support. My journey has not be easy but tell me who's journey has.

To my readers: Thank you for your continued support, allowing me to take the time before going into a place I no longer dwell in to give you these testimonies. I pray that if I could prevent one person (soul) from the madness it will be a blessing.

Chapter I

Rikers Island Correctional Facility

April 11, 1995, It was now that I had become Antoine's Wife and the journey had begun; It was time for my husband to "Pay the piper" in other words (reap what you sow) and of course I went for the ride. I was in a very cheerful mood because I had finally won the man that I had been in love with for the last ten years and he was officially mine. There was no turning back on my decision. I was ready to stick it out until death do us part.

I went to Rikers Island and I got on the line to register for a visit with my husband. It was very crowded, as usual, and I had been tired from the day before. Even though it was my wedding day I had been through so much just to get married that I was not feeling good physically but I was in good spirit. I got to the visiting room and waited for Antoine to come down. When he arrived we kissed and he was just as excited to see me, as I was to see him. We spoke about what would take place in the next few weeks, like him going upstate and me only being able to see him once or twice a month. We also spoke about when he reached his destination, for us to put in for something called "Trailer visits" (those are family planned visits for three days, and they are not always on weekends).

It was not easy getting the things we had planned, such as (a house, his recording deal, children and everything we had dreamed of). All those things would be placed on hold. I looked at my husband and said, "Fifteen years! I will be old if I wait." Antoine and I laugh; we tired to make the best of it. I had no idea what a struggle it would be. As I kissed my husband and enjoyed my visit we both laughed and joked with each other, until it was time to go. Leaving was the hardest thing for me to do. So after my last kiss I would say "See you later!" I never turned around. I made sure never to say goodbye. I think that would have been too much for me.

I went to see my husband three times a week and I eventually met other women visiting their loved ones; I hooked up with this girl that visit her loved one. Her name was Evelyn. She was a Latina from Puerto Rico. Evelyn was cool and she "Rock," which meant that she was (true to the game and the player) just like me. Evelyn was just more open with her hustle. I was very discrete. I knew about moving and packing (cocaine) and had my own clientele but Evelyn moved (dope). I went with her uptown to the Bronx near Third Ave and Willis. One day after visiting my husband, I went with Evelyn as she was picking up Dope in what's called bundles. The bundles were Dope wrapped in white paper, Evelyn bought them in stacks of 12. Evelyn explained that moving Dope was a lot more money than Cocaine. After her pickup we both went separate ways for that evening and to meet another time.

Afterwards I went on home and waited for Antoine to call me so that he would know I arrived home safely. When he called, we spoke and he asked me where did I go today after the visit. I explained that Evelyn had to make a stop and what it was for. Antoine was very upset but I paid him no mind. The same routine took place for about two months. I would go to work and after work, three times a week, I'd go to Rikers Island to see my husband. Later I would put money in Antoine's account, send food packages, clothes, robes and slippers.

On Saturday I went to see my husband and met up with Evelyn after. She and I got together and we just talked about the different things that we do; so as I explained to her about the "Coke" game she explained to me about the "Dope" game. She also confided in me that she supplies her husband with Dope in the prison and that she knows lots of "CO's" (correction officers). Evelyn seemed like she knew a lot of people. She always spoke to the van drivers that took us up to the prison. I was amazed at what she knew and felt honored to know her. But little did I know that she was a "Shyster" (a person that'll take you for a ride but takes your money in the end). Evelyn explained to me that she was involved with inside people that could release prisoner's right from Rikers Island Correctional Facility in Queens N.Y. So I just listened because I wanted to know if everything was Copasetic.

The next Tuesday visit with my husband we spoke about everything that I was learning from Evelyn and in particular about the "Dope" game. Antoine said, "I don't know what you're getting involved in" but he did know that I was trying my damnedest to get him home. So I told him that maybe we should try it to get some real money. Antoine looked at me and said "What have I made you into?" I looked at him and said nothing . He did not know that I had already made an agreement with Evelyn to get him home from Rikers Island. As the visit went on we talked about how I would get the bundles, and he would set up for his deliveries to be brought to him.

Three months later I had finally told Antoine what I was involved in to make the kind of money that I was making. I thought he'd be more upset but he liked the idea that he would never go upstate because I had spoken to Evelyn about the people she had known on the inside to get Antoine out. I believed in her since I saw her talking to those same people in the facility.

I was close to saving the ten thousand that Evelyn asked for but I was still short about two thousand. Antoine was getting "Hot" to the CO's so they began watching him. CO's had a funny feeling that Antoine was involved with selling drugs so I knew that I had to get him out soon.

Evelyn finally told me the date and time that her people were going to release Antoine. I had to do something quick to get the money so I asked my father in law Randy for the rest and he said no because he did not have it. I then asked Antoine's aunt Nadine and she did not have it as well. I ended up pawning all of Antoine's jewelry and mine. My mother Hilda was always a support, she had given me her own memory of my father; her wedding band. I took all of it to the pawn shop. My intension was to get it back before the pawn ticket expired.

It was time to meet Evelyn so that she could finalize the release of my husband by me taking her the cash. Evelyn took it and said she would call me later, I finally felt relaxed about what I had done but I stayed up all night waiting for her call. Evelyn called me the next morning very early and said "Saturday, September 10, 1995 at 4:30am." Those were my orders to meet my husband at Rikers Island. She and I spoke some more and then we hung up. By now, it was the end of August and my temptation was getting stronger and stronger for me to have my husband home. It was about two weeks before his release date. That following

Monday I went to work just as happy as ever, no one could have taken the smile off my face. The next two days I felt good. Evelyn called me everyday asking me, "Are you ready for your husband to could home?." I replied "Yes..".so excitedly! For the next week, I went to work and I visit Antoine, reminding him of his release date and time. The visits were to discuss our future and finally feel like it was actually coming true.

Chapter II

The Day Of Deliverance

On the following Saturday, September 10, 1995, I went to pick up my husband. I waited on the other side of Rikers Island where Evelyn said he would be coming out of. I got there and no one was coming out of the door. It was 4:30 am in the morning, what was I supposed to do? I called Evelyn and her phone was not on. Instead I had gotten the Operator saying "This phone is temporarily disconnected." I was in shock. I've been had. She had robbed me for Ten G's; ten thousand dollars I worked hard for. I started to cry. I had waited about 2 hours in the spot she told me to. I could have gotten robbed, raped or killed. But I didn't even think of that in the moment, all I could do was cry. I decided to get in my car and drive home, to prepare myself to see my husband.

It was now 9:30am and I got ready to get on the visit with Antoine. I was hoping that I would run into Evelyn at Rikers Island so that I could whip her butt! I got on the registration line and had been told that my husband had been transferred Upstate to a new correctional facility. It was called Downstate Facility; that is where inmates are placed until they get clearance from the prison to go to their new residence. It had been surprising to me, I thought that someone from Rikers would have notified me first before moving him but I didn't know what to expect since this was all new to me.

I left Rikers Island in tears. I was now; not in control of my husband's whereabouts. It was devastating that I could not see my husband before they took him. I was in a daze, it was like not being aware of your life. I felt like someone just snatched my joy. I was supposed to be preparing for something like this but it caught me off guard. As I arrived home, I was still in a daze and with plenty of tears. When I entered the house my mother asked me what was wrong. I looked at my mother and said, "Mommy, they took my Antoine. They took my husband away." I bust-out crying and fell in my mother's arms. I did not know what to do being that I did not see Evelyn at Rikers Island to ask about what happened or where my money is. I knew that my mother was going to ask about the money. "Where was Evelyn?" my mother asked. I had finally realized that I had got Played. She had tricked me out of money. I couldn't lie, I had to tell my mother so I got down on my knees and said, "Mommy, I need to tell you something..." and before I could say anything else, my mother said, "I know that you got tricked out your money." My mother then went on to say, "You see Fita, some things are not in your hands. You were so ready for your husband to come home but GOD had other plans. You think that you can change the world but you can't. You must see that for yourself." Then my mother said, "So now that you lost all that money, don't forget my ring. You have three months to get it out." I replied, "I will." My mother went on to ask, "Why are you home so early?" I then broke down in tears again and said, "I had gotten used to visiting him on Rikers Island and forgot that he had to go Upstate." My mother hugs me and says. "It is time that I help you prepare for the journey. I never wanted this for you but I could not stop who you fell in love with. So you need to stop crying and pray for strength."

On Saturday, my mother and I just spoke about the good times that I had with my husband and the bad times. We talked about the beginning of her relationship with my Daddy, the love of her life. My Mother then said to me, "You have to ask GOD to help you. I can only guide you on being a faithful wife but GOD has all control of this matter." Following our conversation, my Mommy went into the kitchen to cook, we ate dinner and just watched movies. My mother was a collector of old movies, after my father died she pick that up as a hobby.

Sunday morning, I stayed in my house and cleaned up the mess I had made during the week. I was hoping that my husband would call. I got my clothes prepared for the week because I always prepare my stuff in advance. My uniform and my civilian clothes both had to be prepared. After about an hour or so, I went downstairs to my mother's house and ate breakfast with her. After breakfast, we decide to go shopping at noon. My mother and I always did the "Girl thing" especially when my best friend Rosie could not do it with me. We spent the entire afternoon having quality time. When I got home and check my messages there were no calls from the correctional facility so I took a shower and got into my bed.

Monday, I got up and started my day by going to work. I did my regular route and went back to the garage to take the truck back and prepared to leave. I took off my uniform, jumped into the shower, put on my civilian clothes and signed out of work. Off I went into the life I had yet to figure out. It was hard trying to go anywhere because I had not yet heard from my husband. So I just stayed local, in front of my house on the porch. My house was just around the corner from my job so it was very convenient.

That evening the telephone rang and it was the recording from the Correctional Facility. There was a collect call from Antoine, "To accept, press one..." so as I pressed one I heard his voice."Hey Mommy" I said, "Hi Daddy! How are you? Why didn't you call me? Why did they move you? Why you took so long to call me? Where are you?" Antoine said, "Baby, if you just stop with the questions, I would be able to answer... Antoine said Time Out!" Antoine started to answer all of my questions. "I am at Sing Sing Correctional." "Where is that?" I asked. "It is right outside of the Bronx, you take the Metro North." I asked Antoine if he was ok and he said he was ok. He was just thinking about me. I replied, "You just take care of yourself in there. I will be fine in the street." Antoine said, "Well, you take the Staten Island Ferry to Manhattan, get on the N train to 42nd Street and go upstairs to get on the Metro North, then get off at Fishkill and it is a few blocks up the hill." I asked what days I could visit because in the correctional facilities they typically go by last name so you have to know the inmates name day(s). Otherwise, you will make a trip and will not get a visit if it is the wrong day(s). Antoine said, "My dates are Tuesday and Saturdays." I told Antoine that I will be there on Saturday. We talked about the things that he needed and clarified for me the things that he was not allowed to get. Then he talked about how much he had missed me and me missing him as well. Antoine then explained the do's and don't's in the prison. Since Antoine was in a maximum security prison, he was very restricted, and the CO'S (correction officers) were not nice because the men in there were doing long-term bids, for some serious crimes.

My husband was a young man. Antoine was 22 years old and was about to be confined for 15 years of his life. It was hard for me to just accept it like that so I would never think of the long time that he had to do. Instead, I took it one day at a time. I was young too, I was older than him but I was still only 28 years old. I thought I was one year older than Antoine when we first met, yes he lied about his age. I was six years older than him. I went to school with Antoine's uncle.

So, on Tuesday, I had requested to switch my chart day (day off). It was approved by the District and the Borough Office on Staten Island. They were very cooperative with my changes. I was the First Woman Sanitation Worker to work on Staten Island. I guess they would approve things for me when they felt like it because most of the time it was not easy. I had to fight a lot of "Wars" to get things my way. Changes are hard to accept, for the Men in the Department it was like giving away their freedom; like looking at and discussing their Penthouse & Playboy Magazines, since they were used to no woman around. But the other fights I faced were race and ethnicity. I was the first woman but also a minority; that was a double shocker to Staten Island.

Chapter III

Sing Sing Correction Facility

I got up in the morning to go on my first visit in the new Prison. I got to the ferry about 3:45am, just in time to catch the 4:00am boat to New York City to hop on the 4:45am N train to 42nd Street. At 5:00am I walked up the steps and on to the escalator in Grand Central Station so that I could catch the 4 train to 125th Street to ride the Metro North train to Fishkill. Fishkill was about four stops on the express train. I arrived at Fishkill at approximately 7:30am. I was very tired and the day just begun. As I walked toward Sing Sing, I felt as if I was going to see the "Wizard." The prison sat right up on top of a hill just a block from where I exited. I thought it was strange how the prison was built. The building was on a dead-end street and was right in the middle of the block. I walk into the building and I started to fill out my paperwork to visit with my husband. I had to show our marriage license, driver's license and a bunch of other forms of ID to verify who I was and who I was visiting. Once I was done I watched the CO call for Antoine. I walk into a big visiting room with many different faces either waiting or already with their loved one. I also noticed a corner vending machine and a separate corner for taking pictures.

The set-up was all new to me. I continued to look around as I waited patiently. I noticed that many of the men were bigger than my husband. From the look of things, they had been in prison for about ten years. I started to get very worried. But even though Antoine was no punk, I was still afraid since I knew Antoine didn't play no mess and did not like to take orders from anyone. I waited about a half hour to see my husband. As he entered the visiting room, tears started to roll down my eyes. I could not believe it; they had cut Antoine's hair. He was bald and in an orange one piece prison uniform that had Sing Sing Correction on the left side of his chest, and some white Skips on his feet. I just fell apart but Antoine seemed fine. He picked me up out of my seat, hugged and kissed me, then whispered in my ear, "Stop being a Punk!" As I hugged him back, I wiped the tears from my eyes and kissed him two more times before the C.O. came over and told us stop kissing and sit down, so we sat.

I tired to get myself together on the visit so that I could actually talk and not cry the whole time. Eventually I did stop. Antoine and I spoke about the two weeks since he left from Rikers Island and of the people he had ran into in Sing Sing that he knew from the streets. One of his cousins was actually in Sing Sing with him. Knowing he had a cousin around made him feel a bit more comfortable. Antoine looked at me and asked, "Are you going to be alright with this time?" I replied, "What are you talking about?" He looked at me and said, "Fifteen years." I looked back at him with tears and responded, "I will take one day at a time." Besides I am fine right now, stop reminding me of the fifteen years. Antoine said, "Ok Bonnie!" That was our little joke (Bonnie and Clyde). Antoine realized that even though he kept the business away from me, he knew now that I could run his business; being that I ran the business from the time that he got locked up and before he went Upstate. After that conversation, we went to get food from the vending machine and took pictures.

We continue to talk and Antoine asked me, "So What ever happened to your girl Evelyn?" I replied "I don't want to talk about it." Antoine said, "You ran for a few months with some business you had never done before and you tell me you don't want to talk about it." "Yes, I don't want to talk about it." I replied, "If you ever let someone run another game on you, I will personally see that the person will not ever stand straight again," he said. I just shook my head and said ok. He wanted me to agree that I wouldn't make any deals without speaking to him first and I agreed. We then spoke of how many times a month I would visit, what type of package he needed and what he couldn't get. We were so engaged with our conversation that before I knew it the eight hours were up.

I felt a little better about what was going to happen for these few months because I had seen Antoine and he looked like he could handle it; "Sing Sing." Before the C.O. came over and handed me my visiting slip, I kissed my husband passionately. I then got up and gave him his quick peck on the lips again and said, "See you later!" and I left. I never looked back.

I visit the next weekend and that was it for Sing Sing Correctional Facility. The next time I heard from Antoine he was in Greenhaven Correctional located in Danimora , New York. Another journey had begun.

Chapter IV

In The Mix

It was October 1995, it was one of the weakest moments of my life. I had been thinking of Antoine for the last two weeks, and to make the adjustment from the train to see my husband to getting on "That big bus" the bus that I was trying to avoid; it was very sickening. Just the fact of knowing that I would be getting on a bus full of women that are angry, and from what I heard, they were always fighting on the bus. Women were always meeting other women that were going to see the same man. I never thought that I would have to get on that bus called "Prison Gap." I had heard of the things that went on in the bus; all kinds of people that get on the bus to see their loved one for miles and a day away. It was like my life was becoming a nightmare. Not even in a million years would I have thought that I would be getting on that bus.

My first step was making a reservation for the weekend to get on the bus. It was so hard to get the reservation; the telephone was always busy. I would try early in the morning, late at night, in the middle of the day, it was frustrating but finally I called about 3:00pm and I was able to get a reservation. I was very embarrassed the first time that I called because they asked me questions that I did not expect them to ask before getting a reservation. But what did I know? I never had to get on a bus.

The conversation went like:

What is your name?

Where you going?

What is the inmate's name? (I was insulted about them calling my husband an inmate.)

What is the inmate number?

Are you his girlfriend?

Are you his wife?

What day are you visiting him?

This is your number when you arrive on 59th Street and Columbus Circle. It will be fifty dollars. Thank you for calling Prison Gap. Then you hear the dial tone, no time for questions about the trip or how far it is, or what time to be there. The Operator must have thought that everyone has been on the bus. She was very rude. I got a reservation for the second Saturday in October, I waited for my husband to call so that I would let him know that I got a reservation, and just to speak to him.

I had really missed him. I waited in the house trying to clean and get myself prepared for the next day. The telephone rang and it was the Operator "This is AT&T calling from Danimora, N.Y. , Greenhaven Correctional Facility, will you accept a collect call from" I hear my husband in the back ground saying "Antoine." I accepted it and was very happy just to hear his voice; it was like having sex (quick) when you hear the voice you love. I was also excited to let him know that I will be coming to see him on Saturday, October 16, 1995. I was scheduled to leave on Friday, October 15th, and be at the bus stop before 10:00pm.

As we were in conversation of what was going on in the street I ask Antoine "What are the dress code requirements for me in the prison?" He said, "No short shorts, no halter tops, no tube tops, and no miniskirts". I said "Ok, thanks for the information, but you know that I was not wearing that stuff anyway. Antoine said "I just wanted to make that clear." I said "So what are you allowed to receive? He said "I can receive 50 pounds of canned goods, no shell fish, no grapes, no rice in a bag, then he went on to tell me that they are not allowed anything red at all; no red sheets, no red pillow covers and he could not get anything navy blue either. So I said "Could you receive a hooded sweatshirt? He said "No." I asked him what was best. Antoine said "Pullover sweat shirts and white shirts with three buttons in the middle, and regular shirts. Then I said "What about pants?" Antoine replied, "As long as they are not navy blue it would be good." I then said "Ok Papi" that was his nick name that I called him, "I will see you Saturday." He said "Ok, goodnight."

We spoke for the next few days. My husband started to spark up a conversation about what was I going to do with my time and I said "I guess I will open up a business or something," Antoine said "Well I have something that maybe you need to consider instead of the business that I left," I said "WHAT!." Antoine said "Relax it's something that you are an expert in. I said "Here we go," then Antoine said "Just hear me out, think about it and on the visit we will discuss it." I said "Shoot" (meaning go). Antoine said "Well I know that you are a formal artist and you sing, dance, and you have an ear for music. I said "Yeah" and Antoine said "Well why don't you open up a company that has to do with the artists?" I said "What do you mean Antoine?," Antoine said "Well I have a guy here that is going to be released in about a month his name is T.J., he live in "Bed Stuy" Brooklyn, N.Y. and he is a good rap artist, he also writes his own lyrics, see what you can do for him." I said, "Antoine I don't know. I will have to spend time with him and I would have to put him in a studio. Then I would have to get his resume done. He would need a full "Press Kit" (8"X10" picture, written resume, and tape with three tracks (meaning songs) done; and that is long hours. With all that to be done it may cause a problem with me not being here." Antoine said "What do you mean?" I said, "You will get mad that I am not home for your calls and then you will start thinking that I must be having an affair." Antoine said, "Look, I trust you and TJknows that I will hurt him bad if he was to try my wife." I said, "I don't know, I will speak to you about this on the visit."

We went on and spoke about the business (his business) and how well I had been doing. How much money was coming in and what I was investing. I said "Well, I have a proposition to make with you on the visit," Antoine said "Here we go!" I said "No Baby, it is a good investment" and Antoine said "You are always coming up with something that I don't agree to, but Shoot." I said "No, I will tell you on the visit". He said "Okay, this way we could have a conversation on the visit that will last us some time." I said "Good." I knew that Antoine was wondering what the conversation would be about and it would be on his mind until the following weekend when we got together, as we spoke on the other things of life. It was about the time that my husband had to get off the telephone because they have a certain amount of time before the telephone calls are disconnected. So my husband said "Ok Mom (that was my nick name from him). Its time, I will speak to you tomorrow." I said "Ok, we both kiss and said goodnight."

The next morning I got up the usual time at 4:30 am. I got in the shower, got my uniform on, and went to work; roll call was at 6:00am. I was more relaxed this morning; I guess because I had spoken to my husband and I knew that I was going to see him at the end of the week. It always felt better when I knew that I was going to see my husband. It was something about the visit that gave me hope to live more. It felt like after every visit I would regain strength and power to continue on for his sake. Antoine always gave me hope; he always made me feel like I was the strongest of them all. He kept me encouraged. After I got my route done I took the truck to the dump. I dumped the truck and took the truck back to the garage. Then I went home, took another shower, and put my civilian clothes on. I went back to the garage and handed my ticket in; see back then we would just get the route up, dump the truck and hand the ticket in. The supervisor was fine with that because the work was complete and the borough office was satisfied that the route was done.

I was always a "Runner on the job" (a person that gets the route up in three hours instead of eight). I always got the route up about 10:30am so that I could do my own thing. I knew that I had to look good for my husband. It had been about two or three weeks that I had not see him so I had to look beautiful on my visit, you know...keep your man lusting for you. So, I went to the Staten Island Mall to pick up something new to wear on the visit. I went into Ashley Stewart because I had gained a little weight during the time that my husband was incarcerated . It's been two years and I have not had any extra-curricular activities (sex) but my hips and butt was expanding. I needed a size 14 Woman. I had finally gotten out of a Misses 12 for sure. I was now in the big league. But trust me, I still had my "Pepsi Cola" shape. By now I was a 38-34-38. So as I walk into Ashley Stewart, I saw this dress and I knew I was going to look good in the dress. It was a dress for the holidays and Thanksgiving was coming up shortly so I decide to get it. That dress caught my eyes from the beginning. It was a drop shoulder (leopard print) collar black velour long dress with one split in the back and it was Sexy!

As I continue to look for something to wear for Saturdays visit, I found this nice Larry Levine olive green pant suit. It was a short to the waist double breast jacket and the pants with the cuff on the bottom, it was" business casual" and that's the look I like because this was a suit you could dress up or dress down. I looked at the time and it was time for me to go back and sign out from work so I purchased my clothes and went to my car (a Toyota Camry) and drove back to work to sign out for the day.

Chapter V

*The Preparation -
Time For The Journey*

The next day I was good. I had gone to work as usual, got my route up, dumped the truck, and took the truck to the garage. It was starting to get cool out and the leaves were falling from the trees. I had gotten a call from a friend of my past that I had not heard from in about six months. She was a very good friend of mine from High School. Her name was Eloise and lived in Brooklyn. She said that she got my number from Rosie so I said it was ok. "Ellie, we have been good friends for years, you don't have to explain where you got the number from. You are my girl from back in the days." Then I said "What up Ellie?" She said "I've lived in Staten Island for a while and I just wanted to see you." I invited her to my house for the weekend because I knew that the following weekend I would be with my husband. So that day we spoke some more about "Erasmus Day" (High School) then we decided that she would come over Friday, I would cook and we'd just have a "Girl's night." It was set. Ellie was coming over on Friday and we would have fun. As I was talking to Ellie the telephone clicked; I had the two-way so I asked Ellie to hold on. I switched to the other line and I hear "AT&T Operator, would you accept a collect call from Antoine?" I said "Yes" and Antoine said "Hello Mommy." I said hey "Daddy" (another nick name); we had many nick names for each other. I said "What up?"; then said "Daddy wait... I got Ellie on the other line." Antoine said "Ok". I got back on the other line and told Ellie that it is my Husband so she said "Ok, I will see you Friday." I said "Ok."

I hung up the phone with Ellie and click over to the line that my husband was on; Antoine said "Ok, who is Ellie?" I said Ellie is my friend from high school. We both attended Erasmus Hall. Antoine said "Is that Ali Ali?" I laugh and said "Yes." He asked "How did she get the number?" I explained that Rosie gave her the number. She lives on Staten Island now. Antoine said "So now you have a partner to be with on the Island." I said "Yes" and I laugh. Antoine asked "What is so funny?" I said "I can't believe that you remember that story about my girls in High School." Antoine said "How can anyone forget that you girls were on the B35 bus going to Flatbush Ave in Brooklyn fighting over Ellie man and everyone on the bus started saying Ali Ali." I think that is the funniest stuff that could ever happen early in the morning. That's something I could not forget about your past". I said "She is coming over this weekend on Friday. He said "Ok have a good time." I said "Antoine, so what up?" Antoine said "Nothing, I just thought of you and wanted to hear your voice." I said "Ok Antoine, I'll talk to you later."

It was now Friday October 8th; it was a week before going to see my husband. I was excited that I was going to see him next week. I was also excited to see my girl Ellie that I have not seen in years, I'd say about five years. I saw her constantly after high school when we were still hanging out but when I left for college the crew broke up. It used to be four of us hanging out tuff; Rosie, Charmaine, Ellie and myself. When I came home from college all hell had broke loose. I mean that there were only two left out of the crew. The only two that stayed down was Rosie and I. Anyway, I was excited to see old true friends.

I went to work as usual and I ran my route up. I dumped the truck, I handed the ticket in to the supervisor, and I went home, took a shower and started dinner for me and my good friend Ellie. I put the ribs in water to boil as I did the same in another pot for my macaroni. I started cleaning my house; it was now about 2:00pm. I went back to the garage and signed out then came back home. That was the luxury of living across the street from where you work. I came back in the house and I continued to cook the baked macaroni and cheese and ribs. I had gone to the liquor store to get some Moet and some wine because I didn't know what she drank but I remembered in High School she really didn't drink nor did I. If we did drink, it was a "Slow Gin Fizz." So, we were all grown up now and I just wanted to have everything covered. I was always a good host so I try to keep my reputation up, you know, the image thing.

It was 7:00pm and the door bell rang. My mother lived on the first floor so I called down to my mother and asked her if she could answer the door. I knew that my mother would love to see Ellie. Then, my mother said "I didn't hear my door bell ring." I said "No mother it was mine, I am having a friend over but I need to go to the bathroom." Please, could you answer my door bell? Mrs. Hilda answered the door and she was in shock! I heard my mother from downstairs; she had screamed Ellie's name. My mother said "Fita (my nickname) Fita Fita guess who's here? I said "Ellie." She said "Yes." Ellie stayed downstairs about twenty minutes just talking to Mrs. Hilda while I continued to complete the thing that I needed to complete before dinner. Then, Ellie came upstairs to my house; I knew that my mother needed that catching up time with Ellie. My mother was one of my friend's inspirations. Ellie came upstairs and I was shocked to see her. She had put on some weight but she looked good. Her face was bright and full of joy! As I hugged Ellie and greeted her with a kiss on the cheek, I invite her into my house. Ellie looked around and says "This is nice" and I said "Thank you." I said "Are you hungry?" She said "Yes" so I said "Why don't we eat first?" We will catch up with the time from the years that we have lost since graduating high school. So as I was fixing the plates, we were talking about so much time that has passed in the years of not seeing each other. Then I served the food. It was perfect and as we ate Ellie ask me where Antoine was. I looked at her and I said "He is still away". She asked "How much time he has?" I looked at her and said this is just the beginning; I have 15 years to be by myself. Her eyes lit up. Ellie said "Are you going to be able to wait for him that long?" I said "I take one day at a time but that is why I do need help and the help comes from GOD." I am looking for a church home but every time I go to a church I don't feel that welcoming feeling that I am looking for. Ellie then said "Why don't you come visit my church? I am "Saved" (Born again Christian) Fita and there is nothing better than living a life with GOD!" I said to Ellie "Ok, I will go with you one day soon". Ellie looked at me and said "Why wait? Come with me Sunday." I hesitated, and then I said "Ok, why wait?" Ellie said "Okay, I will come pick you up at 8:30am on Sunday." I agreed, and then we continued to eat dinner.

Chapter VI

"The Day That The Lord Had Made"

CLC Christian Life Center, Linden Blvd, Brooklyn, N.Y.

It was early Sunday morning, October 9, 1995 about 6:30am. For some reason I heard all the birds sing. I got in the shower very excited about going with Ellie to her church, especially when she told me that all of the people that went to Erasmus Hall High School were attending there. She mentioned that Rosie's cousin Adrienne and Valerie were members at CLC. We all used to be in the same click back in high school. Adrienne was my "Idol"; I looked at Adrienne as a good role model to follow. She was focused and smart; she knew what she wanted just like me. I got out of the shower and I already had my outfit to wear because I had pulled it out right after Ellie had left the night before. It was a navy blue Liz Claiborne walking suit (dress with a long jacket), navy blue stockings and my Nina Ricci blue pumps. I put my hair in a bun, put some eyeliner on my eyes, and put lipstick on my lips. I grabbed my Gucci bag, my beige Larry Levine winter wool coat, and I was out the door waiting on Ellie.

It was now 8:00am and Ellie was soon to arrive. As I waited for her I started to think about the times that I had been looking for a church. The one that I visit did not do anything for me. I was waiting on GOD to touch me because for many years I heard that you would know when GOD is calling you. So I continued to wait for GOD to touch me. I did not know if I was literally waiting on GOD to touch me or when you feel the spirit in a service that GOD was touching you, or if your feet started to tap or if you felt something in your spirit, that it was GOD touching you. Ellie had pulled up it was the first time I had ever seen Ellie drive. I did not think she would ever drive and she did not look like a driver but Ellie had a nice car. I believe it was a Honda Accord or something in that family. I got into the car and I said "Good morning Ellie" and she said "Good morning Fita." I said it is a good morning and she responded yes it is. Then we just started to talk about all the people that attended the church that went to Erasmus Hall High School. After that we started talking about the artists that attended the church and who had visit the church. I was told that Salt from the group Salt and Peppa attended the church and the rapper LL Kool J comes from time to time. It was just nice to go to the Lord's house; something I had not done in a long time. So as we drove off from the front of the house I was just taking the ride in and the more she drove the more we talked about the love of God. As she drove on the Verrazano Bridge I start to have this funny feeling in my stomach. I was not sure if it was the menstruation thing or I was getting nervous that I was going to church. As we got onto the Belt Parkway I was thinking about how many people I was going to see that I have not seen in a long time; about 15 years or more. Then I was thinking about how I could really explain this love for GOD that I had to my Husband. It did not bother him that I went to church but he did not even believe that there was a GOD. He always thought that if there was a GOD, then why did he have to do time (Prison). He never even believed that if you live by the sword, you die by it. It was really hard for me to believe that Antoine really did not believe in GOD. In the midst of me dating him I really thought that he was playing around about his non-belief.

As we got off the Belt Parkway on Rockaway Avenue I started to get really nervous because I knew we were close. As Ellie drove down Rockaway Avenue toward Linden she slowed down and she said we are here Fita, I looked at the building and I was shocked it was the old "Key Food Supermarket" building right across the street from J.H.S. 275; the junior high School from the 70's.

Ellie started to look for parking and I started getting very nervous, my stomach started cramping bad and it felt like someone was pulling my stomach tissues out from inside of my stomach. As Ellie parked she said "Are you ok Fita?" I said "Yes" and she said "You look flushed" I said "No, I'm ok." I got out of the car and I just followed Ellie to the door. When I walked in I was so amazed at how this church was built on the inside; the multi-color of the inside was amazing. The church was two levels; nothing that could have been imagined in a store front. There were three different entrances to the church. It was like a triangle to the pulpit and the pulpit was straight in the front.

Ellie and I were walking to the front when I noticed Adrienne and then Valerie noticed me. I saw Tanya and a few others from Erasmus but I just continued to follow Ellie. As we decided to sit in the third row, they introduced the Pastor. I was very shocked to see it was my friend Kim's sister Karen's boyfriend. When we were growing up and hanging out in Bushwick Projects, his name was Bernard but now he was "Pastor Bernard." I was just amazed at what GOD had done for him. I then spoke to Ellie and she had said that Bernard and Karen had gotten married, so Karen was the First Lady.

Pastor Bernard started to deliver the word of GOD and it was like something had got inside of me that I had not felt before; it was the deliverance of God; it was something that I was looking for but I never felt it in my life. It was an experience that had taken control of me. I started to dance and tap my feet and before I knew it I was in the front of the alter delivering myself to "GOD" I had been SAVED! It was an amazing feeling and it was indescribable. After the service I had to fill out some paper about bible study and they had given us something to drink. I had walked out a new creature; a new person of GOD!

I had left out of the church looking for Ellie, so that I could go home. When I found Ellie she kissed me on my cheek and said "May God bless your walk." I said thank you and I did not yet understand what I was going to go through but I was ready. I got in the car after being approach by all of the people that I had known and the ones that I had not known, blessing me into the "Kingdom of GOD." After getting into the car, Ellie and I sat for the drive home. As I got in front of my house, I said "Thank you Ellie for a beautiful Sunday" she said "You are welcome" and then she said "Have a safe trip going to see your husband next week." I said "Ok, thank you."

It was now about 3:00pm and I went in the house and I sat and spoke to my mother. She asked me questions about the service and I explained to her what had happened. She looks up and said "Thank You JESUS." I stayed downstairs because my mother had already had her dinner done, so why would I go upstairs to cook? There was no one there but me. I ate and watched a movie with my mother. By the time I went upstairs it was about 8:30 or 9:00pm and of course I was waiting on my daily call from Antoine. At 9:00pm sharp Antoine called and he asked me how my day was with Ellie in church. I explained to him that it was great! I did not get into much detail because I needed to get prepared for work Monday morning and I needed to have some good information to speak to him about on my visit so we talked about all the other details of my busy schedule, work and what my schedule looked like this coming week. After that it was time for his call to be over; it was now about 10:30pm so we both kissed over the phone and said goodnight.

Chapter VII

The First Week of Christianity

It was Monday morning, the first day of my Christian walk. It felt as though I had released my heavy burned on God. I had mentally felt light as though I had no worries in the world. I got in the shower got dressed in my uniform and I headed out to my job; which was across the street and around the corner... Literally. I got to work in good standard time for roll call, got my ticket from the supervisor and I went to the Section to pick up my partner. The Section was another building that the department had for sanitation workers to meet their driver. I pick-up my partner and we went to the route. We started doing the route and in a matter of about 3 hours we were done. I drop him off at the Section and I took the truck to the dump. After dumping the truck I took it back to the garage parked the truck and gave my supervisor the dump ticket.

I went home, took me a shower, I cleaned up my house and took me a nap. I woke up about 12:00pm so I ate some lunch and then I went to the garage to wait for sign out and see what shift I was going to get for the next day. It was looking good; I had 6:00am to 2:00pm for the next day. I really didn't care what they gave me because I had already put in time off for the weekend; so that my plan to visit my husband would not get ruined. So I thank God that he was watching my back, especially now that I had given my life to "Jesus." Everything was looking right.

I went home and I got in my car. I drove to the mall just to see if I could find something I like. I did not see anything in a couple of the stores that I looked in. When I went into Macy's, in the mall, I saw this olive green suit that really drew my attention so I checked to make sure that it came in my size. Then I looked for a shirt to go with it and some shoes. I did not find shoes in the store but I had a pair of shoes in my closet that would go perfect with the suit. So I bought the suit and shirt and off I went to the Cinnabon stand. I bought me a cinnamon roll with all of that yummy frosting. I love those rolls and that's why I don't go the mall often; because I am hooked on those cinnamon buns. Then without hesitation I got my butt out of the mall and went back home because I could not wait to talk to my husband about what happen to me on Sunday at church. I was feeling good and full of joy. I felt as though I was dreaming. I walked into the house 4:30 or 5:00pm. I knew my mother would be home soon so I decide to call my mother on her new cell phone that I had purchased for her, but of course she never answered the phone. The phone just rang. Finally when she got home I said "Mommy I called you to see if you want food from the diner and to see what you feel like eating, but you did not answer your phone. My mother responded "Fita the damn phone was in my pocket book, I don't hear it ringing and I don't need everyone knowing my whereabouts at all times; that's all a cell phone is for. I said "Mommy you are bad, it's for an emergency." My mother then looked at me and said "Was there an emergency?" I just laughed as said

"No Mother." We continue to talk and order some Chinese food from the Chinese restaurant.

Chapter VIII

Greenhaven Correctional Maximum Facility, Stormville, NY (Town Of Danimora)

The weekend of my first visit to the new facility had finally arrived. Friday was the day that I was waiting and longing for. As I prepared to see my husband, I had packed my Larry Levine double breasted olive pant suit and my Victoria's under garments, with my black leather Fendi boots and my jewelry. Of course it was now a little cold so I also packed my long shearling coat because I was told that Upstate was much colder than in the City.

I put on a brown velour sweat suit and my beige riding boots with my flight jacket (leather beige and brown jacket). I went downstairs, kissed my mother and then got into my car and drove to 59th Street and Columbus Circle where I would get on the bus to see my husband.

Friday, October 15, 1996 at 10:00pm I arrived at 59th Street & Columbus Circle. As I waited for the bus to take off on my journey (the trip) to the new prison that my husband was now transferred to, I was in a daze (daydreaming). I could not figure it out; What was going on in my life? Or, if I could do this? How long, how many more years? Those were the questions in my mind.

As I boarded the bus, the bus driver said "Hello are you visiting an inmate?" I just looked at him; I always had a problem accepting what they were called. So I said "No, I am visiting my husband." The driver responded "Ok ma'am." As I got in the seat that they had assigned to me, it was along side of the window. It was perfect for me because I wanted to see where I was going and I did not want to talk to anyone. I just did not feel friendly; when the last person got on the bus the driver said "Ok, this bus is going to Greenhaven, Watertown, Elmira and Wyoming.

The first stop will be Greenhaven. This is the prison that my mother told me about, she said there was always a cloud over the prison. She said that it was going to look spooky. I asked her how did she know and she said "This is the prison that your father was in." I looked at her and before I could say anything she said "This is the life I did not want you to see but I could not tell you anything because you knew it all." As tears came down my mother's face, she said "I will have to help you with this walk because it is not easy," then she walked away.

I could never forget the look and the tears that my mom had that day. Anyway, I was prepared for the clouds; I was looking out of the window as the bus continued to move and as we got out of the City I could not figure out where we were and it was very dark. I remember going towards the Bronx and into Yonkers but then I did not know where we were. It was now about 2:00am in the morning and I could not believe that we were still in route to this place. It was a long ride and I remember tears coming down my face. All I could think about was why "GOD" had to take him and why so far. I continued to cry and I woke up the woman that was sitting alongside of me; she started talking to me so that I would feel better but it did not stop me from crying and questioning GOD! I said "GOD, WHY me? What have I done?" I continue to cry and cry even louder until I had woke up most of the women that was on the bus going to see their loved one. I guess I was the only one there that was taking that long trip for the first time; these women had been on this bus before. The woman next to me said "It will be alright once you see him" and I said "No, I just can't believe that it is so far". The woman next to me took my head and put it on her shoulder and said "You could cry on my shoulder if you need to" I said "Thank you."

It was now 3:00am in the morning. The bus driver said "Ok we will be at Greenhaven in about 40 minutes so prepare yourself for your departure." Then the bus driver said "You will have to stay in the waiting area for 3 hours; the facility does not open until 8:00am." I looked at the woman next to me, she said "It will give you time to get prepared for your visit" I looked at her and I said "4 hours? That's a lot of time." She said "No it's not, you will see." Then I said to the woman "Thank you, but what is your name? I have been crying on your shoulder for two hours and I don't even know your name." She said "I am Marie," when she said Marie I heard an accent; it was from either London or Paris. I said "Hello Marie," Marie said "Hello Rafaela" I looked at her and said "How did you know my name?" Well my Dexter knows your husband Antoine and I knew who you were when you got on the bus. What gave it away even more was all of the tears. My husband told me you had never been up here and I was the one who told my husband what bus comes up so that your husband would be able to tell you. For some reason I felt comfortable with

Marie, she was so genuine. I knew, just a feeling in my soul that she was not lying about anything; we continue to talk and I was feeling a little more comfortable. I just started preparing my bags to get off the bus. I did not say much about my life or my husband's life because I need to talk to Antoine about her and her husband. A person like me that had so much going on needed to make sure that they checked out. I was a woman of many hats; it just depended on the day and time. Now, the time had arrived for us to get off the bus and it was 4:00am in the morning. As I got off the bus Marie said "And the race begins." I did not know what that meant, but I eventually found out that it meant that it was time to run and get on line for a bathroom to get yourself together for the visit.

Greenhaven had two bathrooms and it was about forty women and about ten men to get on visits.

The four hours felt like twenty minutes; it was crazy you had to scream or fight to get time in the bathroom. The women there were acting like they had not taken a shower before the trip. They were in the bathroom for thirty minutes or more washing their private parts and getting all dolled up for their men. So I decide that when I got in the bathroom I would generally take my half an hour too. As I was getting myself together I started to cry, I could not believe that I had fallen into a life I never saw myself living; you know the "Mrs. Fabulous, the Queen that I thought I was. It really hit me that I would have to deal with people, personalities, attitudes that I had never in my life imagined. Marie heard me crying and asked me to open the door. I was already dressed so I open the door. Marie saw me and said "It will be alright." I wiped the tears and walked out the bathroom, but in my mind I said "GOD, please help me do this!"

Chapter IX

Registration

It was now 8:00am, the room that we had walked into for the registration was big. The Correction Officer handed me a paper to fill out. This paper had all kind of questions that you needed to answer. The questions were:

What is your name?
    What is your address, city, state and zip?
    What is your number?
    What is the inmate's name?
    What is the inmate's number?
    What is the inmate's date of birth?
    The next paragraph was questions for the visitor:
    What is your number?
    What is your address?
    What is your date of birth?
    Who are you to the inmate?
    What are you leaving today for the inmate? Money?
Food package? Magazine? Books? Pictures? Clothes?
    Have you been here before?
    Are you are married to the inmate?
    Mother of inmate?
    Father of inmate?
    Inmate's children?

Inmate's Brother?

Inmate's sister?

And, in the very fine line it said (if you are married and it is your first time visiting, please have your marriage certificate. Thank you for visiting at Greenhaven).

I was amazed at the questions and how they run a correctional facility, so as I answered all of the questions I was a little bit overwhelmed and tears fell down my eyes again.

I felt like they had invaded my private life. I handed in the form and then I had to wait until the CO (correction officer) called my name. I started to look around and I saw women in clothes that was not appropriate, but who was I to say anything. As I waited I saw women getting denied visits and saw women arguing about things that I had no idea about but it was my first time so I did not involve myself. I'm usually the one that try to make peace but I did not think it was best. Then, a C.O. came over to me and asked me if I was Rafaela Barbour. I said "Yes," he said "Could you come over here?" I was scared but I went. He said "You need to give us your certificate of marriage; we have to get a Copy." I said "Sure, but is anything wrong officer?" he was kind and said "No Mrs. Barbour, it's just standard procedure." I said "Ok."

I never forgot his kindness; his name was Officer Kelly. He was an old Irish man with black hair, tall and thin. You could see that he was a little prejudiced, but he was very respectable with me. Officer Kelly came back to me and said "Is this your first visit?" I said "Yes" he said, "You go down toward the right and you will put everything that you are going to leave him in that room; in a bag. Then you will be searched and they will take his stuff in the roller to him and he will come right down. So I followed the instructions of the C.O. (Correction Officer) then I went into another room after they searched me.

The room was a big room with tables; four chairs to a table. There were vending machines at the right side of the room and on the left there was something set up for pictures. There were also two bathrooms, men and women, and on the side there was door that led to the courtyard for visits.

It was now about 10:30am, I was tired and very much overwhelmed. So, as I waited, I dozed off because the visits Upstate are all day visits from 8:00am to 3:00pm. Mind you I had been up since 4:00am getting ready on this line to the bathroom and then the standing process; I was beat. (tired). I woke up when I heard someone whisper in my ear "Hey Momma." It was my husband, the man that I have been waiting to see for a month and I had not. I was so HAPPY!!! I jump up and I hug him and kiss him and the tears roll down my eyes. Antoine said "Stop crying" I said "I can't believe that you are so far from me." I started crying hard because in my mind I could not believe that GOD would send him so far. As I continued to cry the C.O (Correction Officer) said "Mrs. Barbour are you ok?" I said "Yes, it's just that I have missed my husband." I stopped crying because I did not want the C.O. thinking my husband had done something to me and mess up our visit. I got myself together and I cleared my eyes. I hugged my husband again so tight that I could feel that he was about to break down; I felt his jiggle. I know that he was hurt that he had done this to me; Leaving me alone. Once I got it together I spoke to my husband and Antoine said "So tell me; all "sarcastically"; about your experience in church. I know that you were happy." I said "Yes, I got "SAVED.""

Antoine said "What?" I said "I am "SAVED"" Antoine said "What is that?" I said "That's when you give your life to Christ." Antoine said "So what do you do when you give your life to Christ?" I said "You learn day by day how to live right."

Antoine said "What does that mean? You are going to give up smoking cigarettes?" I said "Yes, it is going to take one day at a time." He said "Well if it'll get you to stop smoking those cigarettes then I believe it is a good thing." I said "I have to read the Bible, learn what GOD is telling me and I needed to get "SAVED." I need GOD to help me with these 7-14 years without you. I want to be focused so that I don't lose my mind." Antoine said "Whatever you say, you will be smoking cigarettes next week anyway." I said "You are stupid, you don't understand and I don't know how to explain it to you." Antoine said "Did you meet your "Christ?"" I said "No! I know he is alive." He said "You sound like the Muslims; they never met Muhammad". I said "You need to believe in GOD, he is the only one that could help you". Antoine said "Yeah right, why am I here if there is a GOD? My GOD is you! All I see is you for me." I said "Please, I am not your GOD." Antoine said "So when I need something, who will bring it to me?" I said "Thru God I deliver." Antoine said "So all I see is you when I need something; my GOD is Mrs. Barbour." I just looked at him and said "I am not your GOD! We should just talk about something else."

I asked Antoine was he hungry and he said yes so we got up and went to the vending machine to get those buffalo wings and french fries; that was about the best thing in the vending machine beside the cheeseburger and hamburger. Then we got some Pepsi soda and sat back down, ate and started to talk about all that had happened in the month that I had not seen him. Before I could even realize, it was time to go, so the Correction Officer said "Visits are over in 20 minutes." At that time I said "Thank you for having someone look over me on the bus." Antoine said "Who got you?" I said "You do."

Antoine said "So how was she?" I said "She was cool." He said "I'm not saying you have to hang out with her but I knew she would watch over you on the first trip." I said "Thank you my dearest Husband." I kiss him a few times and I said "See you later" he said "In two weeks and put money in for the picture department so we could take pictures" I said "Yes Daddy."

As I walked out I never looked back, I went through the gates and started to walk toward the front and then I saw Marie.

Marie said "How was your visit?" I said "Good." She said "I told you that you would be fine"; we walked outside of the prison and I saw that it was dark and so I looked up; sure enough my mother was right, Greenhaven had a cloud hanging over the prison. It was time to get back on the bus to go home and I was very tired. I got on the bus and I talked to Marie for a while. She was talking about where she was born and how long she has been in NYC and how long she has been coming up to the prison. Marie continued to speak and by the time she stopped it was half the ride home. I was tired so I told her I was going to take a nap. Marie said "Ok." I said "Thank you once again Marie" she said "No problem." I was about to nap that when I heard the bus driver say get prepared for your arrival at 59th street and Columbus Circle in 15 minutes. I could not wait to get into my car and drive home. I was very tired and overwhelmed; but happy.

Chapter X

Back to Life

It was now time for the hustle and the bustle; getting into my car, going to the house, getting my stuff ready for Monday morning. The same old thing. When I was with Antoine it was like being on a vacation, it was like everything was right. The moment I left Antoine, it felt like going into another world. Life was different when I was in his presence, I was like the Prima Donna, and he was my King. He treated me special, I was all he looked at and I was the only one he saw. We just spend a lot of time with each other laughing and talking about what we share and have done together. It did not feel like he was in prison. It was different, I really enjoyed my visit. He had given me some inspiration to continue this walk of "Wifehood" while he was away.

It was something about Antoine that I loved so dearly. His words, the way he gave me hope, the love that we had. I loved this man with all of my heart. I started to pull up in front of my door, I got my stuff out of the car, and I went into my house. Of course I stopped at my mother's house and spoke to her briefly. It was now about 10:00pm and I had to unload my stuff from the car and prepare myself for Monday morning.

I did mention to my mother about Greenhaven; it was just as she described. Hilda had described it to be a prison with a cloud over it; regardless of the weather, it always had a black cloud over the prison. I went upstairs by this time. It was now 11:30 pm and I was just getting myself ready for the morning. I took a shower to relax after the long trip. I laid my uniform out for the morning. I got in the bed and the alarm went off at 5:00 am. It was now time to jump in the shower, get dressed and make role call by 6:00am. It was definitely a blessing that I worked right across the street. If I did not work literally across the street, I would not have made it to work; not after that trip.

As I walked across the street I got to roll call on time as usual, I got in my truck and I went to South Avenue to pick up my partner. We got on the route and we picked up the route (garbage). Then I dropped him off at the garage and I took the truck to the dump. The dump was Arthur Kill in Staten Island, where all the "Mules" (Sanitation workers) go to dump a lot of garbage. After I dumped the truck I went to the garage, parked the truck, gave my supervisor the ticket and then I went home to rest. I was so tired from the trip that I need to get back in the bed until it was time to sign out. Most of the time, I would go back to sign out after my nap and then go back to the house. This time I decide to go see my girl Rosie. I need to talk about my trip to the big house. It was something that I did a lot. I would go and chill with my peoples in Brooklyn, so as I was driving across the Verrazano Bridge I was blasting my music because it puts me in a zone. R Kelly had the album "Twelve Play" so I just listened to this album because it would remind me of my husband, Antoine was swift with his voice, and he had dedicated this album to me when he was on Rikers Island.

As I came off the Verrazano Bridge into Coney Island, on the Belt Parkway, I continued to listen to R Kelly. I looked in the rearview mirror and there was a car following me. I did not know who it was but I continued to fly down the parkway. That was something about me; "I get busy driving", especially on the parkway. I open up the engine!!! I usually get off at Rockaway Avenue on the Belt Parkway for Rosie's house but I needed to know if this car was really following me so I got off on Pennsylvania Avenue, the exit after Rosie's house. There it was again, the car followed me off and pulled on the side of me. It was a silver Benz with silver chrome rims and in the middle of the rims it was a Benz logo. When I look on the side of me it was this young, handsome, black man but he did not look familiar to me so I said "Excuse me but are you following me?" (I know that most of you would have not done that but I was a hustler's daughter and wife and I was not afraid at all of anything that would come my way.) The young man said "No, well yes," I said "Well, why?" he responded to me "Are you a Cop? (Police Officer)" I said "Why?" He said because you were doing about 80 mph. I said "So are you a Cop?" He said "Maybe," I said "Yes or no." He said "I never saw a woman drive like you before. I also said that because all women don't drive the same. I'm going to ask you one more time. Are you a Cop?"

I said "Maybe." Then he said "Ok, my name is Cory" and I said "Ok Cory, are you a Cop?" He said "I am a Police Officer and I saw the way you were driving and you changed lanes so smooth that I wanted to know who you were." I said "Cory I am Rafaela and I am a Sanitation Worker on Staten Island" He replied "I did not know that they had women on Staten Island" I said "I am it." He said "What do you mean?" I said "I am the only woman and the first to be stationed on Staten Island." He said "Congratulations." I replied "Thank you" Cory said "Is that a wedding band on your finger?" I said "It is and I'm happy," he said "You don't give a brother a chance" I said "There is no chance."

Cory said "Well where is your husband?" I said "He is on tour." (I know that it was a lie but it was not his business; Cory was a Cop!) Cory then went on to say he knew it was too good to be true. I said "Ok, so are you going to give me a ticket in your civilian car or am I done now?" Cory said "No I'm not going to give you a ticket, but be careful." I said "Thank you." He said "Can I call you some time?" I said "No." I continued to drive to Rosie house.

When I got to Rosie's house she was surprise to see me. She had not seen me in about 1 month. She knew I was going to see my husband so she said "How was it?" and I said "Wonderful!" I went on to tell her how far it was and how I cried the whole time and about the girl that I had met. We talked about how the prison was, then it was about 6:00pm and my cell phone rung; I knew it was Antoine because I had forward my house phone to my cell phone. I accept the call and Antoine said "Hey Momma" I said "Hey Daddy, what up?" He said "What you doing?" I said "Talking to Rosie," he said "On the other line or in person?" I said "In person" he said "Oh, you are in Brooklyn?" I said "Yes" he said "So you forward the phone?" I said "You got it" he said "Tell Rosie I said Hello. What time will you be home?" I said "About 8:00pm" Antoine said "I will call you at 8:30 ok?" I said "Ok," he gave me a kiss and I kiss him back over the phone. I then went on to telling Rosie what had happened to me on the way to her house and she said you know that you always distract men, you are sharp all the time; and your swagger with what you do. You don't drive like a woman and your mind is always ready, that is something that men find competitive. Rosie then said "What are you doing next weekend?" I said "Nothing" she said "I have a babysitter, do you want to go out?" I said "Sure" she said "When is the next time you are going to see Antoine?" I said "We agreed to once a month so I will be going in November." She said "Ok" and we just started watching TV and before you know it was time for me to leave to meet my deadline call. As I started to leave I said "I love you Rosie and I love my God children." I went down to Rockaway Avenue onto the Belt Parkway, took the Belt Parkway to the Verrazano Bridge, went through Bay Street and made my left onto Victory Blvd. I drove up a few blocks and into my parking spot. I ran into the house, knocked on my mother's door, screamed "Hello Mommy" and told her I will be down when I finish talking to my husband. She said "OK Fita." I ran upstairs and it was exactly 8:30pm when the phone rang and I accept the call. My husband said "Are you home?" I said "Yes" he said "Ok, where is Mommy?" I said "Downstairs" he said "I need to talk to Mommy." I went down to give Mommy the phone. I knew that was just his insecurity and he just wanted to know if I was at home. After he finished talking to my mother, Mommy said "Fita come get the phone" so I went down to get the phone. As I took the phone from my mother I started to walk upstairs and Antoine said "So did you enjoy your visit?" I said "You know I need that because I need to see you from time to time. You keep me motivated."

He said "And you give me hope." So as we continue to speak about our visit Antoine said "Will you come November 10th?" I said "Of course, is there some special happening?" Antoine said "No, it's just that I know Mommy birthday is

November 18th and you want to be with Mommy on her birthday. Then, after that is Thanksgiving so I need to get my visits in before the Holidays." I said "You right." We continue to speak about the good time that we had. It was about 10:00pm and the phones shut down at 11:00pm so Antoine said "Mommy I'm going to hang up. I know my boy wants to call his wife too so I told him I will give him some of my phone time. I say "Good night and I love you" and we hung up. I got in bed.

For the next two weeks my life was as usual; I went to work, went home, cooked, cleaned, and talked to my husband about three times a day. Of course my phone bill was always a lot of money but it kept the both of us happy. I spent a lot of time with my mother; we had a lot of quality time. My mother was special to me; she was all I had in my life. She helped me come around with this situation that I was in. My mother made it seem as though it was no different than most married people. Hilda made it easy for me. Hilda, my dear mother, was like my coach. I love her dearly. I also had enough time to party with the girls; partying with the girls was not going out to clubs, just hanging out at their house or staying up late. Sometimes we did go to clubs but we were so much into shopping and just chilling with each other that we did not need to get into men problems. Rosie had her man but our time was ours. It was not always girls night, I was always with Antoine so when I found the time to be just a woman without so much on my plate I would do things like go shopping with my girl Rosie.

It was now getting close to me going on the "big bus" to see my husband. It was the Thursday before and when Antoine called he said "I hope that you are fine but when you get up here I really need to talk to you about what we discussed about a month ago." I said "Ok Baby, don't call me early on Friday because after work I need to get my nails and toes done, I want to get my hair done, so; call me about 9:30pm. I should be done with everything and I will be near the bus by 59th Street and Columbus Circle. Antoine agreed and said "Love you, good night" and I said "Good night."

It was now Friday and I had the long weekend off from work. I got up, went to the nail salon, and I got my nails and my feet done. I called my goddaughter Molisha, she was the only one that I would allow to do my braids and I was going to get my hair in braids. She answered her phone and said she would be ready at 12:00pm. It was about 11:00am so I started to go to her house from the nail salon so that I could get my hair done and be finished by 4:00pm. I needed to get something new. I would not be caught with the same clothes at all. I never wore anything twice; I always had to look good for my husband, nevertheless for myself, that was just me.

I went into Macy's and I pick up this Guess jeans pant suit. It was straight leg with pockets on the side of the thigh and it was a high-waisted with double buttons. The jacket was three quarter length with four pockets; two in the front near the waist and two on the breast with leopard skin just on the collar. I had picked up a leopard print shirt also; I was going to rock that with my miscko leopard boot shoe. I went home and I packed all of my stuff in my "Louie V" travel bag along with all my toiletries, undergarments and my perfume. I decide to spray Pablo Pacso and wear my Adrienne Vittadini leopard skin three-quarter jacket. I took a shower and I threw on my Phat Farm red sweatsuit and I threw on my White high top Gucci sneakers with the red and green stripe down the back. Then I threw on my red leather goose. I jumped in my candy apple red 4Runner truck and started to go to 59th and Columbus Circle. When I got there I parked the truck in the overnight parking, two blocks from the bus stop.

Chapter XI

Business Talk

Friday November 1, 1995

I got on the bus and I went to my appointed seat. I just looked up and said "GOD please guide me on this trip because I am going to see my loved one and I need to get there in one piece. Thank you GOD for giving me all that I need for this trip and forever." That was my prayer every time I had to go on the bus because I heard the stories that these buses break down. It was now cold in the city and if a bus broke down, there is nothing worse than a vehicle out of service. No heat! I am like a baby; if I get cold I start to cry.

People where boarding the bus and I noticed Marie, I called her name and said "Hello Marie," she said "Hello Rafaela"; I loved to hear her call my name, the accent was cute. I said "What is your seat number?" so she said "40" I said "Ok, I will see you when we stop." she said "Ok." As the bus was now full, the bus driver said his little speech.

This is Prison Gap bus company and we are going to Greenhaven, Elmira, and Wyoming prison. If you are on this bus and you are not going to these three prisons then you are on the wrong bus, all aboard.

When the door closed I decide to take a nap between 59th Street and 34th Street where they stop to pick up food or any one of the last items that you need before they get on the road to the first prison which would be Greenhaven. As I close my eyes I heard a loud noise. It was some women that were arguing about a man that they both were going to see. I could not believe the argument and they were not going to stop. I said in my mind 'this is going to be the last time I get on this bus'. I will ask Antoine for the directions and maybe I will drive up. As the girls were still arguing I went to the bus driver and I said "Are you going to stop the bus and straighten out this matter?" The bus driver said "If they decide to fight I hope that they can balance themselves because I'm not stopping!" I looked at the bus driver and said "You are senseless." The bus driver then said "Alright girls, cut it out." I walked back to my seat and kept my eyes open just in case I would have to move.

When the bus stopped at 34th Street I got out. I wanted a coffee and something to eat so as I was walked Marie called me "Rafaela" I turn around and said "Yes" Marie said "What are you going to eat?" I said "I don't know." Marie said "Well, down the block there is a Chinese restaurant. I'm going to get chicken wings." I said "Are they good?" she said "Yes" I said "Ok, I will go with you but I like my wings well done and fried hard." she said "They make them the way you want them." So we walked down to 33rd Street to get wings. As I walked with Marie I ask her "Do you always get on the bus?" she said "Yes, unless I can make a reservation with the "Rosie's Door to Door"" I said "What is Rosie's?" She said it's a woman that started a bus company door to door a few years ago when her husband got locked up. He has 25 years to life. My eyes lit up and I said "What!" Marie said "She is a Puerto Rican lady by the name of Rosie that owns her own door to door Van Service." I said "Are you serious Marie?" she said "Yeah Mon," I said "Does she come to Staten Island?" she said "I guess she does all five boroughs", Marie said "She has like three vans" I said "Could you give me that number?" Marie said "Sure." As we got to the Chinese restaurant we ordered our food and Marie said "When we get back on the bus I will give it to you," Marie said "Why do you think I always look evil on this bus? I hate taking it."

I said "Marie, how much is the van service?" Marie said "It's about five dollars more than the bus, but you get door to door." Marie and I got our food and started to walk back to the bus. As we got closer to the bus a fight broke out with the very same two women that were on the bus arguing. Marie said "This is why I don't like this bus. I ask Marie "How long have you been coming to see your husband?" Marie said "Snce he was sixteen" I looked at her and I said "How old is he now? She said "Twenty-one." The tears just came down my eyes and I said "I am sorry" she said "Thank you Rafaela." I said "I am honored to be in your presence, "How did you take on that heavy responsibility?" she said "When you love someone you just don't think about it you just do it." The statement she made just blew my head and here I was thinking I had the worst of them all. I am here discussing real time with her about other people. I just got on the bus and I said "Marie I will see you when we get there" because we did not have seats together.

I got in my seat and the conversation that Marie and I had just kept rotating around and around in my head. I could not imagine at such a young age to have to do this. Here I was, 30 year old, and I just conversated with a twenty-one or twenty-two year old responsible young lady that has been in this life for five years. I just could not imagine it. Marie took me for a ride. I ate my food and tried to go to sleep but I could not get pass my evening so I just kept my eyes open and watched the scenery.

Forty minutes before arriving, the bus driver would turn the light on and announce "We will be arriving at Greenhaven in about forty minutes, please be ready to depart. Thank you for riding with Prison Gap and have a great visit. I will be back at 4:00pm." I started to grab my bags and I look in the back to make sure Marie was woke and I said "Marie lets rock and roll" she just looked at me and said "You crazy girl," in her English accent. We got off the bus Marie gave me the number for Rosie's (door to door service); I grab it and said "Thanks."

We got into the facility and start to go toward the bathroom so that we could be first to wash up and get clean for the visit. I went into the bathroom and I started to wash up and put on my clothes and in a reasonable amount of time before the other buses come with more people that are visiting their loved ones. By the time I had come out it was about 6:50am and so I sat on the bench inside of the facility to wait. Marie came out after me from the bathroom. Marie said "Rafaela, how long have you been coming Upstate?" I said "Not long at all. My husband was in Rikers for 2 years. This is his first trip Upstate, besides Sing Sing and Downstate." She said "So it's all new to you?" I said "Yes. I am a Newbie."

Marie then asks me "What type of work do you do?" I was more comfortable with her so I said I am a Sanitation Worker for the City of New York. She said "You are making Big Bucks" I look at her and I said "That's what they say." Marie then smiled and said "I'm glad to have met you." I said "So am I"; we laugh and waited for our names to be called for the visit. As my name was called I went to the

C.O. waiting for me to go through the scanner and I went into the waiting area to wait for Antoine to come down. I was very tired by now; I just put my head on the table and dozed off.

It was now about 9:00am and I heard a whisper in my ear. It was my husband, the man that I came to see; this man was mine and I loved him unconditionally. I heard him say "Mommy" I said "Daddy and I jumped on him like I had not seen him in a decade; but that was the love that I had for him. Antoine said "You look stunning" I said "You do too with your jumpsuit on" Antoine said "You see, that's why I love you; you turn gray skies to blue." I said "Pimping ain't easy" Antoine said "So who the pimp?" I said "Me, I know where my piece is at all times" then Antoine said "I know where mine is at all times too." I said "You right." Antoine then asked me how my experience was this time and I explained that it was not bad but I will be driving from now on. Antoine said "I don't want you to drive by yourself" I said "I won't be." He said "So who are you driving with?" I said "Marie," Antoine looked at me and said "So you and her are friends?" and I said "I like her."

I began to tell him our experience and Antoine looked at me and said "I know why I hook you up with her. I know that she is faithful to her husband and I did not want my wife talking to the wrong people." I thanked him. He said "Do you think I would have had her look over you on your first visit on the bus if I was not sure of her and him?" I said "You right." So Antoine asked "Did you ask Marie yet?" I said "No, I wanted to confirm this with you." Antoine said "I'm good with that."

We kept on talking; Antoine said "So are you ready?" I said "Ready for what?" Antoine said "For my proposal." I said "Oh boy, let me get some food first" So we went over to the vending machines and bought wings, french fries, chips and soda. Antoine always wanted his Snickers bar so we got one then went to the table to say hello to Marie and Dexter. After that we sat down and Antoine and I ate. Then he hit me with his proposal. Antoine said "What are you going to do with all this time on your hands?" I said "What do you mean?"

Antoine said "I have 7-14, can you do that time?" I said "Why don't we take one day at a time?" Antoine said "You are beautiful, young and vibrant, smart, beautifully shaped, pretty face, good job and no children. You're married; but I am in prison." I said "So what" Antoine said "How are you going to do all this time without being busy?" I said "What are you talking about?" Antoine said "You need to open up a business to keep you busy." I said "For what?" Antoine said "Look, I understand that you want to be able to have time for me but 7-14 is a lot of time for you to have free." I said "Are you scared that I might find someone else?" Antoine said "No! I know the kind of woman I married; I researched her back ground. Her mother and father were married till death will do them part. "So no" I'm not worried."

Antoine said "From a Man to his Woman, if you ever decide to cheat let it be Bill, Bob, or Harry." I said "What do you mean?" Antoine said "If you have several man friends there will never be a true relationship. If you continue to see Bob, Bob, Bob, then you will build a relationship." I look at him and said I understood. Antoine said "That's not why I said it." Ok Antoine, get to the bottom of this conversation. Antoine said "Well, you are a formal Artist and you have a degree in Business. Why don't you use it to open up a Management Company? You're good at contracts and numbers, you speak well, you have that gift of gab, you are street smart and book smart, you have an ear for music, you are a theater major, you know about unions in the business, you're a great singer and you dance your butt off. What more do you need to know about yourself?" I looked at my husband and said "So what do you have in mind?" Antoine said "There is a friend of mine that is going to be released from here in December. He live in Bed-Stuy and his wife is Puerto Rican. He also has a baby boy. He spit like Tupac and he is very good at "MC"(Rapping). He writes his own lyrics. His name is T.J." I said "So what you want me to do?" Antoine said "He has no money, take him to the studio, get a press kit ready for him, and then get him a record deal." I said "Antoine that is a lot of time that I have to put in with this man and I don't want any problem with you" he said "I'm not worried. TJknows what up." I said "I don't want you to complain about me not making visits because of something with the business." Antoine said "I won't. I said "Ok, I will try something soon. I will try to be prepared when he come out." He said "Thanks Bonnie" I said "Yeah Clyde." So that was the proposal for a Management Company in the music industry. Antoine said it and I do what I do. I understood that clearly. After our long discussion about the new business that I was to open up, I just continued to kiss and enjoy my stay. There was about an hour left so we just kissed and fell asleep in each other arms.

When the visit was over I got up. Antoine said "I will call you a 10:00pm." I said "Ok." I kiss him and walk off the visiting floor. I never look back; not ever. I walk off the visit and I saw Marie and I said "Marie are you coming in two weeks?" she said "Yes" I said would you like to drive up with me?" Marie said "Yeah, that would be good." I said

"Ok, give me you number and I will call you." She said "Kool!"

I got on the bus and I went to sleep. I was very, very tired so I covered myself up and went into a deep sleep. I woke up when the bus driver said we will be at 59th Street in 20 minutes. I then got my stuff together in my bag and waited to get off the bus. Once I got off the bus I walked to the parking lot that I had my truck in, I got in it and started to drive home. I knew it was going to be one of those nights that I had to get my stuff prepared and try to get some sleep to get to work in the morning; and on time.

When I reach home my mother had mention to me, Fita you know it was Victoria's birthday yesterday. I said "Mommy, I realized that after I got on my visit with my husband. I will call her now." I put my stuff on the floor at my mother's house and I picked up the telephone to call my niece Holly (Victoria was her middle name) and I wished her a Happy Birthday. She said thank you TiTi (Spanish for Aunt). I know you were with Uncle Antoine. I said "Did you have fun?" she said "Yes," so we got to talking about what she did and I hear my telephone ringing so I ran upstairs to answer it with my mother's phone in one ear and mine in the other. I hear the Operator say "Would you accept a collect call from... and I hear my husband say Antoine. I accepted the call and told my husband that I was on the phone with his niece Holly because it was her birthday yesterday. Antoine said "Let me speak to Holly" so I put the two phones together and all she could hear him say was Happy Birthday. Then I got back on the phone and Holly said ok TiTi (Auntie) I will let you speak to Uncle Antoine. I will call you later. I said "Ok, thanks. I love you." She said "I love you too TiTi."

Then I got on the phone with Antoine and we continued to talk about the business. I said "Baby, I got to go to sleep. I work in the morning. I love you and I will talk to you tomorrow." I hung up the telephone and started to pull my uniform out for the next morning, I got in the shower and I went to bed.

Chapter XII

Back to Reality

It was now Monday, November 4, 1995 and it was early in the morning when I decide to think about what Antoine and I discussed on the visit. I don't know why it struck me that early in the morning. Maybe it was because I am a formal artist; and I did enjoy the life of the theater, but I had never considered it in the midst of being married to a man that was always financially talented with his business.

I got up to take my shower, as some thoughts came to my mind I was considering it very hard. I got dressed and I went to work. You know sometimes your mind starts working early in the morning when your body doesn't want to; so that was happening to me this morning.

I went to work, got my route up, took the truck to the dump and I drove the truck back to the garage. I gave the dump ticket to my supervisor and I went home. I started to think more and more about the conversation with Antoine. I was thinking that it could be a good idea. I started to put some ideas together about how I would start this little entertainment company.

My body was sore so I ran hot water in the tub; I just wanted to soak in the tub for about an hour. The trips to see my husband where exhausting, it was almost like a weekend trip, well it was, you leave on a Friday and you come back Sunday evening. You're sleeping on a seat for a day and your body is very uncomfortable; so I needed to soak.

I got in the hot tub, my eyes just closed; I had fallen asleep in the tub and it was 'bout 12:30 or 1:00pm by the time I got out of the tub. I started to move fast because I knew that I had to get back to my job to sign out and I wanted to see my shift for the next day. It was not like I had a regular shift. I was the lowest person in seniority. I was on Staten Island and them boys had a lot of time on the job. I was blessed to get transferred close to my house, so my shift always changed. I got to my job to sign out, of course I was on the 12:00am - 8:00am shift which meant that I had to work tonight so I could not do anything too long because I had to get some rest and get back to work at 12:00 midnight.

I drove to the book store, Barnes & Noble in Staten Island Mall to purchase a book that was titled "Business Management in the Music Arena." It was just to brush up because it had been so many years since I had gotten my degree and I knew that thing had changed. I just wanted to be more updated on the business. I bought the book and I went home. I could not get into much else since I had to swing a 12 to 8 shift; I needed rest. I read the first two chapters and I cooked some dinner, then I went to my mother's house for about 2 hours to discuss my visit. I spent some time with her, but even though she lived downstairs from me, I like to sleep in my own bed. I stayed until about 6pm and said "Mommy I have to work at 12am so I need to get some sleep. My mother always understood, she knew I had a lot on my plate, so she said "I will see you tomorrow when I get off of work" I said "Ok Mommy, I love you and have a good day tomorrow at work." She said "Ok Fita.

I went upstairs and I laid across my bed until I fell asleep. It was now 11:00pm and I got up to get dressed. I went on to work; that evening I did relays (taking trucks to the dump.) so it was not so bad. After my last truck I went home to sleep until 8am. I went back to work, signed out and back to the house. At 10:00am the phone rang, it was my husband. I heard the Operator, "You have a collect call from... I heard my husband say "Antoine" and I said "Yes I accept." Antoine said "Good morning." I said "Good morning to you." I said "How did you know that I would be home?" He said "I notice that every Monday you are home because after your weekend it seems as though you swing 12-8 shift." Antoine said "I just took a chance to call." I said "Good observation my husband, you must know my schedule better than me." He said "I do."

Antoine said "Sooo! Have you been thinking about what I spoke to you about?" I said "Yes. I will try to open up a business." Antoine said "Good decision." I said "So, what's the guy name?" He said "His name is "TJ"(Artist) and he will be getting out in December. So maybe after the holiday you could start working with him." I said "Yes." Antoine said "He writes his own songs and he needs for you to take him to the studio, get his press kit done; as far as his resume in the business, and pictures." I said "Ok, that is a lot of time and money so don't get mad if I am not home for your call." Antoine said "I won't be, but you have a cell phone." I said "What does that mean?" Antoine said "You could just forward all the house calls to your cell." I said "Damn, you have all the answers. So you have to be on your game." Antoine always knew what that meant. We continue to talk about the plan for the business then Antoine said "Well in two weeks it will be Mommy's birthday (November 18) so I know that you will be home with her. So that leaves you Thanksgiving to come up." I said "You are so slick!" He said "You don't want to spend Thanksgiving up here with your husband?" I said "Antoine, I would not miss it for the world!" and I laugh. Antoine said "That means that you did not plan to do that." I said "that was my plan; I just wanted to surprise you."

Antoine asked "How are you coming up? Are you driving?" I said "I think I will but I'm not sure because it's on a Thursday. I don't want to be tired, you know I work Friday so I might call that door to door service Marie told me about." The lady's name is Rosie. He said "Ok just let me know." I said "Ok then." Antoine said "Ok Baby, I will let you go to sleep and I'll call you later; Ok? Love Ya."

I went back to sleep because it was still morning, actually early afternoon; and I had all day to just relax. I woke up about 2:30pm and I called my job to see what my shift was. The garage supervisor said I was going 4 - 12 so I just said "Thanks." and I hung up. I had a break; I did not have to swing 12 - 8 again so I just laid back in bed and decided what I would cook. I tried to cook a good warm meal when I had the chance and besides, I wanted to have a meal for my mother. I decide to cook chicken and rice with corn. I called my mother on her job and I spoke to her. I told her I would pick her up because I did not have to work until tomorrow at 4pm so she said "Ok Baby, thank you." I told her that I would be there about 5:30. She said "Ok Fita."

I decide to get up and start my dinner. As I was cooking my dinner the phone rang; it was the Operator, "Would you accept a collect call?" I accept the call and Antoine said "Hey Baby." I said "What up?" He said "What are you doing?" I said "Cooking." He said "What are you cooking?" I said "Chicken and rice with corn." He said "Mmmm, sounds good. Are you working tonight?" I said "No, 4 - 12 tomorrow." He said "Are you going to pick Mommy up?" I said "Yes." He said "Ok, well when you go to pick up Mommy please see if you can get some of my food package together so that you could send it to me; I want lobster." I said "I know that what you always want your seafood." "I am a seafood eating you know what." Antoine said. "Right? When I am eating...." I said "Never mind, because I don't have time to go thru this right now." He said "I can't get none?" I said "No." He said "Why?" I said "I don't have a lot of time right now."

Antoine and I use to have a lot of phone sex. I know where he was going; he expected me to start talking dirty so that he could play with himself and I could play with myself as well, but I have to finish cooking and go pick up my mother so I stopped him before he could get started. Antoine said "Ok, when I call you tonight just be ready!" I said "Ok.", because it was going to be on and popping.

Antoine started to talk about TJ (Artist), when he gets out of prison, how I was going to master the business and I continued to explain my plan. After we finished talking it was about 4:45pm. I told him that I had to go get Mommy but I thanked him for talking to me while I had finished cooking. He said "No problem, that's why we are a team." I said "I love you and I'll talk to you later." He said "I love you too Mommy", and we hung up the phone. I made sure the stove was off completely and I put on a black turtle neck, my black Moschino jeans, my timberlands boots and all my jewels (Jewelry).Then I put my Gucci flight jacket on and jumped in my truck to go pick up my mother. My mother worked in the boro of Manhattan in N.Y.C but I went thru Brooklyn (Boro in NYC). I drove out of Staten Island and onto the Verrazano Bridge to the "BQE"

(Brooklyn Queen Expressway) to the Manhattan Bridge. Then to my mother's job; she worked on 58th Street between 2nd and 3rd Avenue.

After getting into Manhattan to pick my mother up; there was always traffic, as usual, getting out of the city. So we went to Brooklyn until after rush hour. I love the boro of Brooklyn. That was my old stomping grounds. All my people were in BK (Brooklyn). In Brooklyn there was not a lot of women that accepted me, so I did not have a lot of woman friends. I had mostly male friends; women could not handle what came out of my mouth. Especially women that were not about anything; women that sat at home waiting on a man was not one of my Peoples. I speak truth and some women could not handle the truth. I was very raw with my mouth. I was a "Realist" before a "Woman" and I know that real things happen and women could not handle me or my mouth. The ones that had been down with me for years; they were the same way. Otherwise the only other women that I was around were my family members.

I got to my TiTi Lou (aunt) house and I dropped my mother off there until the rush hour was over. I went to see my girl Rosie to shoot the breeze. We talked about everything that we have not spoken about in a month and of course about the business that I was going to open up.

Rosie said "I think that's a great idea. It will keep you busy." I looked at her and said "Do I need something else on my agenda?" She looked and said "Hey, why not? You are multi-talented." and I said "Yeah right" with a smirk on my face. Rosie just laughed.

It was now about 7:00pm and I said "I have to go Rosie." She said "Ok, see you when you come back for the weekend." I said "Ok." I went to pick up my mother at my aunt's house and we went home. As I got into the door of my house I surprised my mother with dinner. She ate and was very content with her meal. I went upstairs to my house and I got in the shower. Then I got my night gown and I put on the bedroom stereo CD player with my favorite artist, R. Kelly's Twelve Play album. I waited for my husband to call about 8:30pm because I was going to blow is mind tonight with some phone sex.

It was now 8:30pm and the telephone rang; on time. I knew it would be my husband so I answered the telephone and waited for the Operator to say "You have a collect call from..." and I heard Antoine say "Daddy" and I said "I accept" and Antoine got right to the point. He said "What do you have on?" I said "Nothing." I know he was stuck when he heard that; he choked. I said "What up?" He said "You don't have anything on?" I said "NO!" He said "Touch my vagina." I said "I am." I continued to rub it then he said "Rub it until your wet." I said in a soft voice "Anything else Daddy?" He said "Stick your finger inside?" I said "How far?" He said "As far as you can." I said "And now what Daddy?" He said "Stick it in and out, in and out Mommy until you release what has been inside you. That's what you have been missing." and I said "Oh Poppie!" He said "Oh Mommy!" and I said "Are you touching it? And he said "I have been touching your penis since I got on the phone and I'm about to release some stuff that I've had since I seen you." "Oh Mommy!" I heard him say. "Ooh, oh Mommy!" and it was quiet. I said "Antoine" he said "What?" I said "You alright?" He said "Yeah, just finishing." I said "Ok was that good!!!" He said "Hell Yeah, and for you? I said "Yes!"Antoine said "Mommy I got to go. I'll call you right back." I said "Ok." And we hung up the phone. It was 9:30pm and I knew that the phone will cut off at 10:00pm so I just waited. About ten minutes later the phone rang, I heard the Operator and I accepted the call I said "You ok?" He said "Yes, I just had to go clean up." I said "Ok." We continue to talk about a half an hour about our experience on the phone then it was time to hang up. I heard Antoine say "I love you." I said "I love you too." then the line got cut off. I went to the bathroom and took a shower and got in the bed relieved. It was my first experience with true phone sex; actually doing this thing they call "Masturbation".

The next morning I got up about 8:30am, I fixed breakfast and lay in my bed until about 10:00am. The telephone rang, it was my husband. I accept the call and Antoine said "Good morning Mommy?" I said "Good morning." he said "What you doing?" I say "Lying in the bed." He said "What you have on?" I said "Nothing." He said "So you have to work today at 4:00pm?" I said "yes.' He said "Can I have some?" I said "Yes." I lay with my legs open and I said "What do you want me to do?" He said "Touch it softly." I said "And then what?" He said "Rub it, the middle of my vagina, and then take your other hand and play with your breast." I said "Oh Daddy! He said "Yes Mommy, I love you and I and I love you too." He said "Is it wet?" and I said "Are you hard?" And he said "I'm hard as a rock!" I said "Ok Daddy, rub my penis up and down, up and down, and let me know when you are putting it inside of me." He said "Oh my, I'm coming." And I said "Good Daddy, because I am too." I said "Let me hear you moan my name." He said "Oh, oh Mommy I can't stop!" I said "Let me have all of it Daddy." I heard him scream and so did I; I was full enough to release. It was now about 11:00am. Antoine said "Call you back." I said "Ok." About ten minutes later he called and I accept the call. Antoine said "You like it?" I said "Yes"; and we both started to laugh because we never thought we would see ourselves in this situation. He said "Thank you for being my wife." I said "Thank you for being my husband." We talked about an hour more and then it was a little after noon. I said "Baby, I have to get in the shower and prepare to go to work." He said "Ok Baby, I love you." I said the same and we hung up. I got in the shower and I got myself ready to go to work. I went to work feeling so relaxed it was not funny. I must have been very sheltered for years, I pick my partner up and I work on the route like never before. I have been rejuvenated! I finish my route and I dump the truck, gave the ticket to my supervisor, went home, took a shower and lay down. It was about 7:30pm so I just lay there thinking of my husband and I having phone sex. I fell asleep and I woke up about 11:40pm and went to the garage to sign out. The rest of the week was the same. I got my regular call three times a day and even some more phone sex. The next two weeks I spoke to my husband on a daily basis. We discussed the business and I even spoke to TJ (artist) on the phone. I continued to have phone sex; it was becoming a regular thing for the both of us. I started to get used to this, accepting what it was.

Monday, November 18, 1995, it was Hilda McEachin (my mother) birthday so I decide to take her to dinner. I invited all the family. We went to an All You Can Eat Restaurant. It had just opened up on Foster Avenue in Staten Island NY. So my brother and his family came from the Bronx to celebrate Mommy's birthday. As I pick them up from the Staten Island Ferry I saw someone from my past that I had not seen in a long time. He was a former acquaintance (Junie) and so we talked. He asks me how I was and I said I am good. He asked how Antoine was doing and I said "He fine." Then I ask him how he was and his family. He said they were good, so I said "Well take care."

He said "Who are you waiting for?" I said "My brother and his family." He said "Ok, it must be a celebration." and I said "We are taking out my mother for her birthday." He said "That's nice. Tell Mommy I said "Happy Birthday." I said "I will." The boat came in and my brother and the family were on the island, so I took everything out of their hands, they got in the truck and we went to the house. It was time for us to go to the restaurant so I told everyone to get in the truck. I had made a reservation for 8:00pm and for a large table because we were going to meet my aunts, uncle and cousin there.

We got to the restaurant parking lot and I got out of the truck to help my mother out; and sure enough my brother got out to escort my mother to the restaurant. I walk in with the kids and my other family members were there. My aunt, TiTi Sarah and her children; it was great. We had a lot of fun! We had a cake brought out to my mother, she was surprised. My brother Junior was always the clown; him and my cousin Leon, so they decide to eat everything. My brother even tried to take a bag full of lobster out but he got caught and we laughed. My mother had the greatest time of her life that day especially seeing that my father had not been there. He had been dead about 3 years. We stayed a little longer in the restaurant but by the time we left my mother was in tears; crying her heart out. She did not expect me to have given her anymore surprises but I had one big surprise. It was a plane ticket for 2 weeks in Puerto Rico. After that it was all she wrote; My aunt Sarah wanted to go to. We returned back to the house, it was very late on that Monday night but I had already requested a change of chart (day off) for Tuesday so I did not have to work the next day. For the remainder of the week my shift was 4 - 12 which was good. I would be going to see my husband and I knew that after the visit I would be working 4 - 12 Friday.

Chapter XIII

The Preparation of Thanksgiving Visit 1995

Greenhaven Correctional Facility

Wednesday, November 25, 1995, it was my chart day (day off). I got up early to get my nails and my hair done. I went to Macy's to look for a special dress for Thanksgiving. I want to look stunning for my husband. It was the first holiday that I was going to spend with him since he has been away in prison but it was his third year in the system; the third prison Upstate NY. He was in a maximum prison (long term) which meant that I had to be very distinctive on what I wore, otherwise you could not get into the visit.

I went to Macy's and I kept looking around. I saw nothing except for this one dress that caught my attention. It was a long black velour dress with a split in the back of the dress, leopard drop shoulder. It was the dress of the century; it was made by "Naomi", the black model. It was off the hook (glamour). I had to have it, so I purchased the dress for $125.00. Then I went down to the shoe dept. to buy a pair of shoes to match it.

I found some leopard pumps, "Nina Ricci" for $ 100.00. I got on the line and purchased the shoes then got out of the store. Then I went to the store to pick up some black stockings. I went to my truck and went home to prepare for my trip. I called Marie to see if she had done all her stuff and Marie was always on point.

We were going to drive up; our first driving trip to Greenhaven Correctional to see our loved ones.

As I drove home I called my best friend Rosie to tell her about the dress that I had purchased from Macy's. Rosie said "Girl, you are going to give those people up there flammer (fashion). I continue to talk to Rosie until I got home I said "Girl I am home now." She said "Ok, I will speak to you after you come back." Rosie said "Happy Thanksgiving." I said "Happy Thanksgiving to you and family."

I got into my house, started to pack my bags and the telephone rang; it was Marie. She said "What time will you come to pick me up?" I said "I will pick you up about 12:00am (midnight)." Marie said "Kool."

"What is your address?" Marie said "I am on Park Place between Utica Avenue and Rochester Avenue." I said "Kool, I will be there about 12:00am." She said "Ok, I will be ready."

It was usually about a 2 hour drive but on the bus it was a 4 1/2 hour trip; stopping at the food stands and covering all other prisons. I had a "lead foot." (I drove very fast) so I would be there in 1 1/2 hours. We decide that when we got to the exit before the prison we would go into a motel to sleep. It was a "Motel 6"; and then go to the prison for 8:00am visits. It was about 1:00pm so I had about nine hours to cover everything that I need to do before leaving for my trip.

My family always spends Thanksgiving in the Bronx with my brother and his family but it was the first time that

I was not going to be there with my family. So, I still had to take my mother and the food that she was going to cook up to the Bronx.

I went downstairs and started to talk to my mother. She let me know that it was going to be different without me. I said 'Thank you Mommy. I love you too." Hilda was always understanding, she said "Well you have a husband and you need to spend holidays with him; when you can." I said Thank you Mom." It was about 2:00pm when I went upstairs to start packing my stuff into my LV (Louie Vuitton) duffle bag. I put my jewels (jewelry) and then I put the dress, shoes, Victoria Secret under garments, and my stockings. I felt like "White Linen" for fragrance, so I stuffed that in the bag along with "White Diamonds". I was not sure what I would want for the visit so then I continued to pack my sleep wear; which were pajamas; for a motel that I was going into with another woman, no need to be sexy for that. I put my lipstick and eye shadow in my bag; I never really wore makeup; I was GOD's beauty. I packed all the necessities, then I covered it with my first 3/4 brown mink coat with a mahogany mink collar; engraved on the inside said "Mrs. Barbour." I folded it up and I put it in the LV duffle bag and zipped it up.

I jumped in the shower and I put on a navy blue Nautica velour sweatsuit with my white high top Gucci sneakers; I was set and ready to go.

I went downstairs to Mom's house to help her with the food and her stuff. She was going to stay the entire weekend with my brother and his family.

My mother enjoyed her grandchildren so much and they loved Grandma when she came to stay. It was about 4:30 -5:00pm when we got in the truck after loading all that we need for the holiday, Mommy and I got in the truck and we set off for our holiday adventure to the Bronx.

I drove down Bay Street into the Verrazano Bridge, then onto the BQE (Brooklyn-Queens Expressway) into the Williamsburg Bridge to the FDR Drive and into the Bronx. As I got into the Bronx I called my brother's house to let them know to come down and help Mommy with her stuff. He was at the door when I got there; as a matter of fact my whole family was down to help. My nieces, Stephanie and Victoria, my nephew Chino, and my sister in law Vicky; we greeted each other with kisses; that's what we do as a family, especially "Spanish family". Kissing each other is a form of respect.

I stayed with my family until about 8:00pm and then I gave my family their hugs and kisses. Then I started to leave. "I need to see my mother-in-law before the holiday", I said "Happy Thanksgiving" to my family and they said the same to me; except my niece Victoria, she was the "Old woman."

"Where are you going?" I said to spend Thanksgiving with Uncle Antoine. She said "Ok, tell him I said "Happy Thanksgiving" and then Stephanie and Chino said tell him we said the same. I said I will. I jumped back in my truck and I headed to Brooklyn to see my mother-in-law Ms. B and my brother-in-law Trevon; just to wish them a Happy Thanksgiving. They lived in the Greenpoint part of Brooklyn on Harmon Street between Wilson and Knickerbocker. I got there and it was about 9:00pm. I stayed about an hour or two and them I left on my way to pick up Marie. It was about 11:00pm and I needed to pick Marie up at 12 midnight. So, I drove down Wilson to Broadway, took Broadway to Utica, made a left and took

Utica down to Park. I made a right and Marie was outside in front of her door waiting.

I pull up and Marie loaded her stuff in the truck; we were on our way. Marie read the directions and I drove. I took Utica to Pennsylvania to the Jackie Robinson to the Interboro to I 678 via Exit 7 towards Whitestone Bridge to 678 North; it became the Hutchinson River Parkway, toward Brewster. Merged into I-84 West (Exit 9w) towards Newburgh to the Ludingtonville Rte 40. Turned right onto Rte 52, slight right onto old Route 52. Then we turned right of the exit and into the Motel 6. It was about 2:30am when we got into the Motel 6.

I registered then Marie and I went into the room. I was very overwhelmed with the entire day. It was a lot to cover, so I needed to take a bubble bath; as I got into the bathtub I fell asleep. I really don't remember how long I was in the tub but I heard someone knocking on the door. I open my eyes and it was Marie, I said "Oh I'm so sorry." Marie said "It's ok; I just did not want you to drown." I laughed and I said "Thank you for waking me up. I would have probably still been asleep." Marie said "It has been a long day for you." I said "Yes."

Marie said "If you want, I could drive in the morning to the Correctional Facility. I said "Ok, that would be good. By the time of our trip Marie and I had become very close, so I had trusted her with a lot of what I had and what I was involved in.

Chapter XIV

First Thanksgiving with my Husband

Greenhaven Correction, Thanksgiving Day,
November26, 1995

It was morning now and we were getting ready for the visit.
I was getting dressed and so was Marie. After we got dressed,
I turned in the key and we started on our way to Route 52.
We turned left onto Rte 216 to Rte 594. Then we took
Route 216, got off and down the road was the Correctional
Facility. It was now 8:00am and we were on line for our
visit. I told Marie "I will see you later. Enjoy your visit." and
Marie said the same. I registered at the desk with the C.O.
(Correction Officer) and I waited for them to call me to be
searched from head to toe and then be cleared for my visit.
Once I was cleared I went into the pool of women to wait
for the men to come down. As I walked into the visiting
room I went to the vending machine to get 4 buffalo hot
wings, 2 french fries, 2 Iced teas, 2 Snickers bars, and I got
picture tickets. This was like a movie ticket but you paid
the C.O. (Correctional Officer) before entering the visiting
floor and the picture guy; which is a man doing time in the
prison that is going to take your pictures.

I went back to my seating area and waited for my
husband to come down. As I was seated I saw Antoine come

thru the gates; being uncuffed. I started to smile; it was a smile that was pasted on my face every time I was with him. As he came close, my insides started to race, it was so hard for me to deal with him being in prison but I never let him know that he had put me in an uncomfortable position in my life. I just prayed because I had GOD with me but I never discussed much of this with Antoine. He would not understand so I jumped up and I kissed my husband. I held him so hard and I said "Happy Thanksgiving" Antoine said "Is everything alright?" I said "Yes."; just like a Trooper (someone faithful).

I then sat down and Antoine said "Well you look beautiful." I said "Thank you." He said "Are you planning to see the President or your husband?" I said "My husband is the President." and he laughed. Then he said "Well the President is horny." And I said "So is the First Lady." So he said "Are you going to get the President anything special?" I said "Whatever the President wants from the First Lady." Antoine said "You are lucky I am locked up but I will try to get up in that dress." And I said "If you succeed then you hit the jack pot!" Antoine said "Look, let me talk about business because I am hard now." And I said "You better because I am wet!" Antoine said "So how was your drive? Good?" He said "So what did you do? Did you drive up here this morning or did you stay in a motel?" I stayed at a motel; me and Marie. "Good" Antoine said. Antoine always asked questions.

Antoine asked "How was work this week?" I said "Good." Then Antoine asked "Did you get mail from me this week?" I said "No." He said "You should be getting a money order from me this week for $300.00." I said "Ok, when did you mail it?" He said "Saturday." I said "Well it probably will be at the house when I get back." He said

"Ok, when you get it it's for the start up." I looked at him and I said "Start up for what? Your business or mines?" Antoine said "You know what; that's for mines." I said "Ok, so I will have to take care of that first and let it turn over. He said "Then I will give you money for yours.

As far as the business, do you have a name?" I said "I think I'm feeling (considering) "Barbour Entertainment". Antoine said "That's nice. I'm feeling that too!" He said "Well getting back to what has to happen, I will be sending home $300.00 weekly and you do what has to done with Barbour Entertainment." I said "Have you spoke to "TJ" (Artist)? He said he will be home early December. I said "Ok, so the first of the year I should be up and running." I said "Am I going to meet him?" Antoine said "When you come back up he will be on the visit with his wife. I will introduce you to him then." I said "Ok Baby." Antoine said "Is all the paper work in place?" I said "I went to get the application for a business number and the business tax number. I made up my business cards and I got in touch with some of my friends that are in the business. I also got in touch with an old friend of mine that works at "William Morris Agency."

Antoine said "Who?" I said "Andrea, she is the first black woman agent at William Morris." Antoine said "I did not know women were in that agency." I said "Yes, she books (assigned) Tupac, Ice Cube and some more artists." Antoine said "So you have everything in place." I said "I will start going to open mics (upcoming artist shows) to recruit and sign up TJ (artist) to perform. I'll start to hook up with the industry events and put stuff on the weekly agenda. I will meet with a friend of mine that makes the "Press Kits"(Resume -Bio) for artists and get in the mix with the small business owners and see what's out there.,

Then I have to set up someone that can promote that's in the business." He said "Ok, sounds like you have it under control." I said "Yes, that's why you appointed me."

Then we spoke about the other business, the business that was my dark side. I had to go uptown on 225th Street and make sure things where done, pick up money and whatever else it required. Sometimes early in the morning on my days off. I liked my life style and it was fine for the moment. I needed to know everything that was going on around my husband. Then after all of the business talk we got up to microwave the french fries and the wings. As we walked, Antoine spoke to Marie and her husband Dexter.

We walk towards the microwave; it was the only time that we would really touch standing by the microwave. It was my favorite; I used to stand in front of him waiting to use the microwave. He'd rub that "Big Old Boy" on my butt; I used to enjoy that so much. I loved to rub up against him. It was fulfilling. I was a married woman with my husband in prison and I was in heat anytime I got around him. When we walked together and warmed up the food it was touch time and I mean that was the only time. I used to feel him up and sometimes we use to have humping sessions by the microwave; we both would deliver our true feelings, he would release and so would I. There was so many people at the microwave that the C.O.s (correction officers) did not see us humping and rubbing up our private parts. Nevertheless, I would also enjoy taking pictures. It was the only time that I got to sit on his lap; so we took pictures all day. But this particular day was a very special day; I went to sit on Antoine's lap for the picture and he had moved my dress up and it had that spilt in the back of my dress. As I went to sit on his lap for the picture I noticed that as I went down I felt my husband's penis going inside of me, he had ripped my stocking. I was surprised but I could not show it and I sat straight down on it. It was so good; I had not felt that in three years; I was in heaven! I continued to just move around and around and I just could not help myself. I was going faster and faster and then the both of us released some of the sweet energy that we had inside of us for so long. I got up and he was swift; he put "Old Boy" back in his pants and it was over. I had finally got some of that good old stick that I had been missing. This was our first adventure like this. I don't know if it was the dress I wore or what but there were so many people at the picture stand that I truly was thankful. I enjoyed my husband having sex with me without anyone noticing; that was the best part. Then after that we went to eat our big dinner, we took pictures again and of course;"it" happened again. I believe that was my Thanksgiving treat. I was revived again and it was on after that day.

The big "Spade" (card) game was next; I'd lose my mind and my body was in heaven. I was ready to just hug and kiss; and that was not allowed much. I learned to get my kisses off when the C.O. was not looking. I started to master how I was going to get what I wanted from him. It was now about 3:00pm and time for us to say goodbye. It was a GREAT visit; but now it was over.

The C.O. came to our table and said the visit was over. I got up and Antoine said "You starting to get real daring." I looked at him and said that I wanted that "Big Boy". Antoine said "You are really starting to get daring." I look at him again and said "See what happens the next visit." "I will see what you are going to do the next visit", he said. I just laughed and said "You keep wondering." and as I got up I kissed him and said "See you." I kept going even if Antoine was to call me back or say something I just kept going; I never looked back because that would have probably killed me. I just kept it moving.

Chapter XV

The Ending of My First Holiday at Greenhaven

As I left the visiting room I asked Marie if she wanted to drive because I just wanted to sleep. She said "Yeah." I said "Thank you." She said "You are welcome, it's no problem." Marie said "I want you to know that everyone in the visiting room just adores you and your husband. We always talk about how well you and your husband get along. I said "For real?" She said "Yeah, everyone talks about how you and Antoine have so much fun." I said "Maybe because I have known him for a long time and we have been together since before he had gotten locked up. I lot of the woman here get with the men in here and they know nothing about them on the outside." Marie said "I guess you are right, but me and my husband were kids together." And I said "That's why you and him get along." She said "Not like you and your husband." I said "Antoine and I have fun; we laugh, sing, and play. We are the same sign (horoscope), we are both Gemini; we know each other in and out."

I finish my conversation with Marie then I went to sleep. I trusted her driving skills so I was able to sleep. I woke up and we were in Brooklyn N.Y. I said "Thanks Marie." She said "Ok. Then she asked "Are you going in two weeks?" I said "Yes, are you going up?" She said "Yeah." I said "I'll see you in two weeks."

I then drove from Marie's house to my house on the Island (Staten Island). I wanted to get in the shower and go to sleep. My mother was not to be picked up until Sunday. I got in the shower and then I went to bed. I was drained but content. I had some of that "Good Old Boy" from my man. I woke up; it was about 7:00am. I didn't have to be to work until 4:00pm so I just laid in bed thinking of what had happened on my visit.

I could not believe that we had actually had sex; I was still thinking about it. I did not feel any way; Antoine was my husband. I got out the bed about 8:00am and I started to fix some breakfast for myself and the phone rang. It was my husband, I heard the Operator say "Would you accept a collect call?" and I just pressed the number one and Antoine said "Hey there, how are you this morning?" I said "Fine." Antoine said "I did not ask you how you look; I asked you how you feel." I said "I feel different." He said "What do you mean?" I said "For starters I am very sore. I have not been on the horse in three years!" Antoine said "But was it good?" I said "Of course, but I am in pain; just a little. Antoine then said to me "So is it that you are questioning yourself about how it went down?" I said "Maybe." Then he said "Well I will never do that again without your permission." I said "Ok, thanks."

Antoine started to discuss the next visit. I told him that I will see him in two weeks and then I would wait until after the holiday to come back up because by then Christmas would be coming and then New Years; so he agreed. We discussed a few more things and I told Antoine that I wanted to take a nap before going to work. He said "Ok my love." and he hung up. It was now 10:30 in the morning so I went back to sleep. I woke up at 2:00pm and I got in the shower to start my day. I got dressed and went to work. I was doing garbage that night so my partner and I got to the route and completed the route about 7:30pm. I took the truck to the dump; I came back, parked the truck and gave my supervisor my ticket. Then I went home to cook my dinner and to watch some TV. About 11:30pm I went to the garage to sign out by 12 midnight. Saturday, I had to swing back; 6:00am to 2:00pm, then Sunday was my off day. Sunday night I picked up my mother and we came home. It was so relaxing on that Sunday because I had covered so much stuff that was behind me and that's when your mind can rest. For the next two weeks I went to work, completed my route, and went home. Of course I talked to my husband everyday and maybe even three times a day. It was just like he was home and he was out in the street taking care of business. It was Thursday night, December 10, 1995, the day before I was to go up to see my husband and I decided not to drive. I was going to try the door to door van service. I called Marie and I told her I was going to try the door to door, Marie said "Ok, I will meet you on the van." I said "Ok." I called and I made a reservation. The reservation was not all detailed like the Prison Gap Bus. The lady answered the phone and said Rosemary's Van Service. I told her I wanted to go to Greenhaven Correctional. She asked for the name and address and then gave me a time and told me the price. She took my number to call me when the van was outside my house. I waited for my husband's to call and to tell him that I was getting on the van on Saturday.

Chapter XVI

Rosemary's Door To Door Van Service

December 11, 1995

Friday morning I got up, took a shower and I went on to work. I picked up my ticket at roll call and I headed for the Section to pick-up my partner so that we could go to the route and pick up our garbage. I got to the route and I cleaned (finish) my route. I took my partner back to the Section and I drove to Arthur Kill where we dumped the trucks on Staten Island. I dumped the truck and I drove back to the garage; I parked the truck and handed my supervisor the ticket (dumping receipt).

I went home to shower and then go to the Staten Island Mall to buy something to wear to see my husband in the morning. I went into a store that was in the mall called "Ashley Stewart". I was 30 years of age and I was a woman filled out in the right places so I was a size 14w (36 34 42) I had some big hips and proud of 'em.

I went into Ashley Stewart to find something nice and elegant. I looked at a black nylon jumpsuit that zippers up from the stomach to the neck, flair bottom; it was HOT! I picked it up then went to see about a belt. I saw a silver chain belt embroidered with diamonds. I picked that up and some stockings and got right out of the store and out of the mall. I got into my truck, left the mall, and went back to the garage to sign out.

I went home to pack my bags. I did not need to go to the nail salon because I had already been there last week and did not need a fill-in. I did not go to the hair salon because I was going to put my hair up in a J-Lo Bun with some white diamond earrings my father had given me as a gift. I did not have to buy shoes or boots; I had a pair of black patent leather boots made by Ellen Tracy that I was going to wear so I was set.

I put all the stuff in my LV (Louis Vuitton) duffle bag and some "Victoria Secret" perfume. It was a pure fragrance. I continue to put all my undergarments in the bag, my white gold jewelry, and my diamond earrings. I pack my makeup bag which included eyeliner, mascara, and lipstick; and of course my long black leather with the black mink collar and my black coach pocketbook. I was now packed for my trip by about 4:00pm. I started my dinner; I cooked some "Arroz con pollo" (Spanish yellow rice and chicken) it was done in about an hour so I ate my dinner and called my mother to tell her I was coming to pick her up. She said she was going out with some of her girlfriends. They was going to take her out; it was a late birthday gift and she would be home tomorrow. I told her that I would be going to see my husband. She said "Ok, then I will go to my sister's house on Saturday and you can pick me up on Sunday. I agree and I said "I love you Mommy. Enjoy your weekend." She said "You tell my son-in-law I love him." and we hung up. My mother, she had a true love for my husband; he had reminded her of my father. It was certain things that he did like, Antoine being a provider; my mother knew that I would never need. Also, the way he was so caring and respectful to adults.

So I decide to go see some friends of mine that live on Staten Island; Yvonne and her cousin Brandy. I threw on my blue Guess jeans and red Guess shirt with my white Gucci sneakers and my red leather Gucci jacket. I did not do my hair; I just threw on a white Guess skully hat. I knew Antoine was going to call at 9:30pm so I had 4 hour to myself. Free time, it was something that I was not used to but I got some from time to time.

I got into my truck and drove to Yvonne's house. She lived about four or five blocks up the hill (Staten Island had high hills). She lived on Henderson Avenue between Winter Street and Jersey Street. As I drive up the hill onto her block I did not see her car but I still knocked on her door because sometimes her mother had her car. So I knock and Yvonne opened the door. I said "Girl, I was going to go on by but something told me to knock. Yvonne said "Ok, my mother has my car." As I went into her house she was cooking but I was not hungry so I just sat and talked while she was cooking. I asked her where Brandy was. She said "At work." Then we talked about some people that she knew uptown in Washington Heights in Manhattan. Yvonne said she would hook it up for me to meet them so that we could do business. These were some Dominican men that were in love with Yvonne and her cousin Brandy and they were in the same kind of business that I specialize in "The Game". I needed to get hooked up because they sold pure weight and that's what I like to buy; it was time to bring the "Loot" (money) home. I had a business to build into a big empire.

Yvonne said "When are you going to see your husband this month?" I said I was leaving tomorrow so Yvonne said "Well let's make it for next week." I said "Ok, kool." We continue to talk about the holiday and what the plan was.

I was going to do it big so she said "You are crazy girl." I said "Yeah; that I am." It was now getting late and it was time for me to go to my house to get my nightly call from my husband so I said "'Ok Yvonne, I'll see you when I get back." She said "Ok Fita, don't forget to let him know I said hello." I said "Ok."

I left and went home. As I walk in the door it was only 9:00pm and the telephone rang. It was the Operator, "Would you accept a collect call?" I said "Yes" and I heard that voice of the man that I love. Antoine said "Hello Mommy." I said "Hello Papi" he said. "What are you doing?" I said "I just got in." He said "From where?" I said "From Yvonne house." He said Is that the girl on Staten Island?" I said "Yes." He said "What is that all about?" I said "Well, I was just taking care of so business." Antoine said "Like what?" I said "I will talk about it on the visit." He said "Ok, I understand. I said "I will be taking the van service. I am not driving." He said "Ok, did you make your reservation?" I said "Yes." He said "So what time does she come?" I said "3:30am." He said "So you will be going to sleep early?" I said "Yes." He said "Are you alright for me tomorrow? (That was sign to let me know that he was going to try to get some (Loving) on the visit) I said "No. I don't think that's a good idea for tomorrow." He said "Ok." I said "Hey I am going to need some money." He said "Ok, we will talk on the visit." Antoine asked "Did you get any mail?" I said "Yes." He said "You need to go to Brooklyn?" I said "No, I will be going uptown to Washington Heights but it will be for next week." He said "Ok, the ball is in your court." I said "Thank you." As we continue to talk about different things it was getting late so Antoine said "Ok Mommy, I see you when you get here." I said "Ok

Papi, I love you. See you tomorrow morning." and we hung up. I got in the shower and then went to bed.

It was 2:00am in the morning. I got up and out of the bed, into the shower, then brushed my teeth. When I got out of the shower the phone rang. I answered, it was Marie. She said "They just picked me up and they are going to pick up another woman then we will be coming to get you." I said "Ok." I put on my Moschino black jeans and a Moschino wool pullover sweater, my Coach penny loafers (shoes), my Coach belt and my leather flight jacket. I got my LV duffle bag and went downstairs to my mother's house. She had not locked her door so I waited in the living room until I got my call to come out.

It was know about 4:00am when I got my call. I got up and lock my mother's door, picked up my LV duffle bag out of the hallway, and locked the front door as I walked toward the van. The side of the van it said "Rosemary's Door to Door Service". The door opened and the driver said "Hello Rafaela, I am Rosemary." I said "Hello." She said "You will be going to Greenhaven Correctional?" I said "Yes." Rosemary was so polite. She was young, about 5 feet 8 inches and she looked about 40 years of age. She was Puerto Rican; She had a "bob hair cut" with studious glasses on.

I was impressed with her hospitality. It was different from the big bus. I got into the van and she had another woman in the front seat that assisted her on the trips. I got on and said "Hey Marie." Marie said "What up?" I said "Just chilling." Then Rosemary started talking to Marie like she knew her like I did.

Rosemary said "Rafaela, I heard so much about you." I looked at her. I said "You have?" She said "Yes, Marie talks about you all the time. I'm glad you finally called for my service." I look at Marie and she said "I always take Rosemary." I said "Ok." So I just sat in the van listened to what was being said and I heard that Rosemary visits her husband in Wyoming Correctional, that was the prison that the bus always goes to after dropping me off at Greenhaven Correctional.

I started to get comfortable; it was just five women and they were my age or older so I knew there would be no drama on the van.

I look at Rosemary, "Is this your van company? Rosemary said "Yes."

How many vans do you have? Rosemary said "I have five."

What gave you the idea to start a van service?

Rosemary said "Rafaela, it is no secret that I have been doing this run for nine years." I said "Why?" Rosemary said "My husband has 25 to life." I closed my eyes and tears came down my eyes. Rosemary said "I was young, just like you and I started on the Prison Gap Bus too. But after a few months I just started to take women up in my vehicle, then I started to invest in a van and I started my business. I get people Upstate safe and I get to see my husband. Then she said "Thank GOD he gave me the strength." So I just sat there crying and Rosemary said "Suck it up and be a big girl. I have been a big girl for a long time and I have not cried for a long time so don't make me get mushy." I said "I'm sorry." She said "You can't help who you fall in love with; 'now can we.'" I looked at her and said "You are right."

I just started to think about her situation. I prayed for her and her family. I continued to just look out of the window while she was driving. I didn't even say anything to Marie because it was so hard for me. I got into this walk of life with the man that I had chosen and asked GOD for. I started to realize that my situation was not as bad as the women that I kept surrounding myself with. I don't know if GOD was telling me to go or that I was in a better place than they were; but I just kept going. I figured if this was not the shoe GOD wanted me to wear he would let me know. But then again, how was I going to know? I had not been back to church to hear any of his Word. I was just living life.

As we got closer to the prison I just started to get prepared to see my husband. <u>When</u> we got to the prison Rosemary said "Ok girl, Greenhaven Correctional. It is now 7:00am and I will be back at 4:00pm. Have a great visit." and she smiled. I looked at her and said "You have a good one too." Rosemary said "Thank you Rafaela." I said "You are most welcome." I got off the bus and so did Marie. The other women were going with Rosemary; their spouses were in the prison that Rosemary's husband was in. I said to Marie "Have a nice visit." She said "Yeah Mon."

I got into the building and I went thru the same weekly process; it was signing in, them clearing my visit, going through the scan, waiting to go thru the door and on to the visiting floor. Then, while waiting on Antoine to come, I was so confused and dazed that when Antoine got on the visit I did not even notice he was in the seat next to me. Antoine said "Hey Baby." I said "Hey." Antoine said "What's wrong?" I said "Nothing, I just can't believe how nice and humble the lady, Rosemary, was that brought me up here." Antoine said "What do you mean?" I said that "She is a woman that is running a van service without her husband." Antoine said "Where is her husband?" I said "He is locked up in Wyoming." Antoine said "Ok, so what's wrong?" I said "It's just that he has 25 to life." and

Antoine said "Oh!" I said "Anyway, can we just get into our visiting?" Antoine said, "That would be nice." I said "Ok, Hey baby. What up?" Antoine said "Nothing, you tell me. What's on your mind?"

I said "Yesterday I went to see Yvonne because she knows some Dominicans that sell weight and I was going to pick it up from them. They are much cheaper with the price." Antoine said "How is the "candy"?" I said "I believe its pure chocolate, but I will see this week when I meet up with them." He said "What are they selling it for?" I said "$40.00 a gram, so I was going to get three grams for a hundred." Antoine said "That's a good deal. Look at you Mrs. Bonnie." I say "Yeah Mr. Clyde, I was taught by the best." So then he wanted to know how it is getting shipped. I said "By Bonnie, there is no third party in this." Antoine's eyes light up and he said "What?" I said "I don't want people in my business." When you get the payment, if it's too much for you to mail, I will pick it up in the ladies room like in the city." He said "Are you sure?" I said "I don't like when I send people up here to deliver and I don't know if it's just a delivery or a friendly visit because it was always women friends that you know; so that's cut (over). I'm running this from now on until you get home! Your other visits are cut. I was hearing about too much stuff going on during the visit to get the "candy" so I am doing what's best." He said "I never thought that you would take control of this." I said "I can't have women all up in my husband's face." Antoine said "Are you sure? I said "Yes."

We continue to enjoy our visit, took our pictures and we went to get the wings, french fries, soda and Snickers Bars. We played cards as usual and then the visit was over. The C.O. came to the table to dismiss us. I got up, kiss my husband and I said "See you later." Antoine said "Fita?" I said "What?" but I never turned around. He said "You are crazy!" I said "You made me this way!" and I left.

It was about 3:30pm so I went outside and then Marie came outside. She said "How was your visit?" I said "Good, how was yours?" She said "Good." And we left it as that. The van came, we got on and we were on our way.

Rosemary said "Did everyone enjoy their visit?" and everyone responded except me. Rosemary said "How was your visit Rafaela?" I said "It was good, thank you." She said "You welcome." I started to fall asleep and before I could really go to sleep I was at my front door. I said "Thank you. Mrs. Rosemary, can you put me on the list for next week?" She said "Sure see you then." I said "Ok, thanks. See you Marie; call me when you get home." She said "Kool."

I went in the house and I just took all my clothes off. I wanted to just relax, it was just a little too much for me to absorb. I got in the shower, went to my bed and went to sleep.

Chapter XVII

Week 2 of the End of the Year

December 12, 1995

On Sunday I went to pick my mother up at my TiTi (Auntie in Spanish) Lou's house and then we came back home. I cooked dinner for my mother and myself, we talked about my visit and then I went upstairs.

The next morning I got up and I went to fix breakfast, the phone rang, it was Yvonne. She asked me what day and time would be good to go meet the men. I told her that I was working 4:00pm to 12:00pm the whole week except on Friday; I will be working 6:00am to 2:00pm. So she said she would set up the meeting for us to go on Friday about 9:30pm. I agreed. We spoke a little more and then we hung up.

It was now about 11:00am when the phone rang again; it was the Operator. "Would you accept a collect call?" I pressed the number 1 and Antoine was on the line. I said "Hey Baby, what up? He said "Nothing, just chilling." I said "What's going on that you are inside and not working out?" He said he was thinking about what I said and he was just wandering if I was sure. I said "I am sure." And then he said "Did you speak to Yvonne?" I said "Yes, I will be meeting her on Friday night. I will see you on Saturday."

There was nothing else to be said about anything or what was about to take place on Saturday morning, so we talked about his food package and money. Then I said "Baby, I want to eat and get ready for work. Call me about 10:00pm, I will be home. I love you." He said the same and we hung up the line.

I went to work that evening and for the rest of the week. I spoke to Antoine the whole entire week and it was now the end of the week and the Friday to meet with the men for the candy. It was about 9:00pm when I went to get Yvonne and Brandy. I did not drive my truck, I drove my Camry uptown and I got to 253rd Street and Broadway. Yvonne said to park on the Avenue so I did. Then we walked to the store. It was easy; it was a grocery store and they sold Spanish food. We went in the back of the store and I was introduced to the Dominican men. Their names were Tony and Demise; they were "Fine"(good looking). The both of them were about 5 feet 9 inches and they were both fry chicken brown complexion; you know the Dominicans have that nice pretty color and they had dark hair.

I said "Hello." Tony said "Hello Mommy" and Demise said "Hey." They both walked into a different room in the store and ask me to come in without the girls. Then the men asked me if I was a Cop. I said "No" then they said "What's your full name and address? I gave them the information and then they asked "Who was I working for?" I said "I don't work for anyone; just me." Then Demise said "Ok, here is your taste." He gave me some candy cola, I put it to my nose and sniffed, it was very strong so I knew that it was good. Then Tony said "Ok?" Tony told Yvonne and Brandy to come in because my test was over and they were more secure of who I was, they quoted prices and I asked for what I wanted. I said to Tony that I wanted 6 grams for

$200.00 and then Tony said "I'm only giving it to you for that price because you are firm, you are about business and you are Boricua (Puerto Rican). We laugh and continue to talk. We stayed a few more minutes then I told the girls that I was ready.

It was late by the time we reached home; at least 1:00am. When we got to Staten Island I had to drop off both the girls. Then, I had to stay up and bag up for tomorrow. I was delivering my first package so everything had to be done right; no mistakes. I weighed it and then I bagged it the way it was supposed to be for this particular delivery. It was stuffed in a blue, red and yellow balloon, tied tight and then I put it in a cool place until I was to leave in the morning. I took a shower and went on to sleep. It was now 3:00am in the morning. I had gotten my call from Marie that they were going to pick me up at 5:00am this morning. There were a few other women that Rosemary had to pick up so I thought; cool it would give me enough time to pack my bag and find a place to keep the produce cool before delivery. I got in the shower and I got out very quick. I went to the closet to get my LV duffle bag and my Versace knitted gray turtle neck dress. I put my square toe Gucci black leather boots in the bag, some Victoria under garments and my jewelry. My hair was going in a bun; I put my makeup and some Blue Jean (Versace fragrance) in my duffle bag also. My bag was packed and now I had to find a sweatsuit to put on. I put on my Baby Phat brown sweatsuit, my Coach sneakers, my Coach bag and my leather flight jacket. It was now about 5:00am and I heard the van pulling up so I got the produce and I placed it in a pocket in my Coach bag. I came outside and got in the van. I said hello to everyone and I sat in the back. I went to sleep until we got to Greenhaven Correctional and then I got up. Rosemary said "I will pick you guys up at 4:00pm." Marie and I said "Ok, thank you."

It was my first time delivering this type of package but I had planned it all out. So I got into the facility and I went to the bathroom. I got dressed, placed the produce in its proper place, and I went to the desk to fill out my papers and wait until they give me clearance to go through the scanner. After the scanner I had to go through the door to go to the visiting floor. I got through all of the process and I was waiting for Antoine; my husband, the man that I adored.

I waited and fell asleep. Before you know it someone was kissing me in my ear; it was my husband. He said "You are tired?" I said "Yes, I did not come from uptown until 1:00am so I'm very tired." Antoine said "Are you alright?" I said "Yes, why?" Antoine said "Well are you then?" He looked at me, I said "Boy I got this, let us go to get your food, go get tickets for the pictures and then lets enjoy our visit," Antoine said "Where is it?" I said "That's not for you to know." He looked at me and said "We are partners at everything." I said "I will tell you later." So we continued to get all of our needs and then we sat down. Antoine and I had a good conversation about the business and what I see coming from this. After our conversation I went to the bathroom and I came out and I kissed him, gave him the product, then got up and went to warm the french fries up and the buffalo wings in the microwave. Antoine got up a few minutes later and went to the men's room. It was complete; I went to the microwave when Antoine came out of the bathroom. He helped me with the food and we sat, the drop was done; I had delivered the package. We talked about everything underneath the sun and before I could take the pictures the visit was over so Antoine said he would get the picture reimbursed.

The following week I went up and I had taken the van. It had become more comfortable for me so I just took the van and I delivered one more package for the last part of the year. The following week was Christmas weekend so I decided to stay home and pick up some gifts so that I could have Christmas with my family and friends. It was more of a home holiday to celebrate and not be stressed on what the new year was going to bring; a lot of hard work for me. I spent the holiday with my family and half with my in-laws. Christmas day my husband called me and wished me a Merry Christmas and a Happy New Year. We talked about the plans for the New Year as often as we could so that we would be on the same page and make no mistakes; there was no time for that in this game.

Chapter XVIII

CEO of Barbour Entertainment

TJ Signs

It was now the New Year, January 1996 and TJ (first artist) was out on the street. It was time to get busy. I had to arrange my shift to accommodate my new business; "Barbour Entertainment", which meant that I had to get TJ in the studio, prepare his press kit (which entailed an eight by ten photo) so that meant a photographer was needed, a resume of his artist influence, and three tracks (songs) with him spitting (vocals). TJ was a "Rap Artist", that is where they spit lyrics about what they have been through; it tells a story. Then I would have to complete the press kit (package that you hand to a recording company for a recording deal) to shop to a record label. That only meant to me that there was a lot of work that had to be done.

I had the long end of the stick, I had to work on my job, and then I had to do Antoine business too; I was the one to pick the supplies up for him, I had to bag the produce, and I had to get to it to its destination;, while Antoine just call the shots. So to prevent any conflict with my job I just signed the night roster. I took the 12:00am to 8:00am, it was called graveyard shift.

The first thing that I did was put together a Manager Contract; to cover myself from any money that I had to invested into this new artist TJ, so that I would get my hard earn money back if TJ was to get signed to a record label. I was taking 20% of all that TJ would make; whether it was rapping, dancing, films, or anything that had to do with the entertainment industry. But mind you, I was footing all the expense. I would be paying the Photographer, I would be paying for studio time and be the person that was going to be putting his resume together professionally. I would also be paying if I had to showcase him at a paid event. I would also be the one putting new clothes on his back for shows. After I got my management contract in order I ordered some business card. These were the things that I could afford, before all the other money started to come in by mail.

I called TJ and I set a day that I was going to meet with him and his wife. I did not want to cause any conflict with the wife so she needed to be a part of this too. I decide to meet them on the weekend, Saturday, January 15, 1996 at their house in Brooklyn. They lived on Pulaski between Troop and Marcus Garvey Blvd.

It was now Saturday, January 15, 1996 and I was on my way to meet TJ and his wife for the first time. She said that it would be better to come upstairs to their apartment and discuss what the Manager Contract entailed. She would cook and we'd discuss the contract. So I agreed that was the plan. As I was on the way to the house TJ called me and asked could I stop by a store and get him some beer and a liter of Pepsi, so I agreed and hung up.

I got in front of the building and I had to call TJ because it was now dark and I was not familiar with the building. He came downstairs to pick me up and we went up to his house. His wife was at the door; it only gave me a sense that she did not trust her man to meet me at the door; opposed to waiting until I got in the house. I found that very strange but I said hello and I introduced myself to her. She said "I am Mrs. Walley." I said "Pleasure." I walk in after her and I sat right at the kitchen table and I pulled out the contract. I explained everything to TJ and his wife. She asked me a few questions about when he goes on tour; where was I going to be as his manager. I responded "Along side of TJ." That was hard for her to understand, I explained it to her and said look we are not going to be in the same room at night so don't think that he even interests me. I am just doing this for my husband Mrs. Walley. My husband took an interest in your husband so you need to shake all those untrusting feelings that you have off. I'm not going to work with him if you can trust him. My husband trusts me and I know that TJ is good looking but my husband is fine!

I then continued to explain the contract even further and she still couldn't understand so I had to stop myself and explain in the language that she could understand. Then I asked is there any questions about the contract and she said "No Mrs. Barbour, I am good with it, thank you for understanding my position." I said "It's ok, I have a husband that is incarcerated and I know how you feel. TJ is just coming home and is going to be around another woman besides his wife, I could definitely understand your position.

I asked TJ if he had thought where there any discrepancy with the contract and he said "No, let's do it!" So that was it; he signed the contract and we ate and celebrated his new contract. It was about 8:30pm, I was ready to leave. TJ walked me down to my car. TJ said

"Thank you Mrs. B." So I was now his manager and it was time to get him started in this business.

I went home and I was tired but I waited for my husband to call. It was 10:00pm and the telephone rang it was the Operator, "Would you accept a collect call from Greenhaven Correctional?" I heard my husband in the background and I pressed 1. My husband says "Hey Mrs. B, Manager of "Barbour Entertainment, Inc." I said "Hey Daddy, what up?" He said "You tell me." I said "Well, I just got home from TJ house. He signed the contract and it is notarized so we are good." Antoine said "Congrats!" I said "Thank you." He said "Well what's your plan now?"

I explained "I have to make appointment with Veronica of Applause Entertainment, She is going to do the bio for me, but I will be taking courses so that I could do my on my own in the future." Antoine said "Good, I guess you have a photographer to take his picture." I said "Yes, I will make an appointment for the photographer in the morning. I will be calling Tony Tucker from Greenwich Photography in Manhattan. He is a good photographer and he is reasonable with his price for an upcoming artist. Then I have to schedule some time at the studio."Antoine asked "Do you have a studio?" I said "Yeah, I have a friend and he recommended a studio in the Brooklyn near Boro Park." Antoine said "Well Mrs. B you have it all set up." I said "Yeah, I got this, this is up my alley." Antoine said "Ok Mommy, I will call you tomorrow because you know that it's 11pm and the phones are going to cut off. I love you, speak to you tomorrow." I said "Ok love you." and the phone cut off.

The next morning as usual I got up and I got in the shower, put my sweat pants and a tee shirt on, went downstairs to my mother's house, and talked to Hilda while we cooked breakfast; like every Sunday. I told her to get dressed; it was our quality time day. We went food shopping and of course my mother likes to go shopping for her house so we shopped for house stuff. Then of course, I brought clothes and shoes; I was definitely a Shopaholic.

It was the end of the day and after all the shopping we returned home. My mother took her stuff out of the truck and into her house; I took my stuff up to my house. My mother decides she would cook dinner so that was the plan; I would eat with my mother. My mother cooked some Arroz con pernil (Yellow rice and Pork shoulder) and a salad. I ate and I told my mother that I would be going up to my house for the night. She said "Ok Fita, I will see you tomorrow." I said "Ok Mommy, love you." I went to my house and I started to prepare my clothes for the week; uniform and civilian clothes. Then I wrote up my schedule for the week; Things that had to be covered, Photographer, call Cathy for the resume, schedule studio time for TJ. I wrote myself a note so that I would not forget what had to be done.

I jumped in the shower and got more relaxed until Antoine called. It was 9:00pm sharp and the telephone rung it was the correctional facility. "Would you accept a collect call from Antoine?" I press the number 1 and I said "Hello Daddy." Antoine said "Hello Mommy." I said "What's going on?" Antoine said "You." I said "What do you mean?" Antoine said "You are what up. I called you early." I said "Oh I went shopping with Mommy." Antoine said "I figured that you forgot to forward the calls to your cell. I said "Yeah, sorry baby." Antoine said "That's ok."

Antoine said "So, what does it look like for you this week?" I said "Well, we are going to get his press kit done and maybe one track at the studio." Antoine said "Ok, so you have a busy week." I said "Yes." Antoine said "Did you get the mail from me?" I said "Yes and on schedule, thank you very much Clyde." He asked "How everything going out in the street?" I said "Just as it should. Everyone is bringing in what has to be in." Have you been on the block? I said "Yes, the block is coming along fine." Antoine said "Anyone give you a problem?" I said "No, not yet, but I guess they know I'm not a nice person or they think I am not nice because I am your other half; and since you were not so nice they probably don't think I am nice, so everything is good."

We talked about my job. Antoine said "This is your last week on days?" I said "Yes starting next Sunday I will be going 12am to 8:00am so that I can keep an eye on all the other businesses I have without having a problem with my real job." Antoine said "Ok Bonnie." We laugh and I said "Baby, it's about 10:30pm and I need to get to bed." So Antoine said "Ok Baby, I will talk to you tomorrow. Good night." I said "Good night Baby." and I hung up.

Monday thru Friday I went to work. After work I drove to Brooklyn to pick up TJ to take him to Veronica in Manhattan to do his resume and to get some photos taken at Allen Tucker studio. It was Thursday; everything was done except I had not covered the studio for TJ to record a song. So Friday evening I met TJ at the studio in Boro Park. It was hard just coming up with a track (music) for TJ so about 6:00pm we called it a night until his next session on Monday morning. It was the end of January and there was so much more to be done but I knew that I could not go on with this business without getting a "Dose" of my husband. So, I had to make sure that I was prepared to see him; he was my energizer, my coach.

On the visit I could get away from the world and it was just Antoine and I. So I decide to go see my husband. I gave TJ twenty dollars and told him that I needed to go see my husband so he could get on the train home. I drove home to Staten Island and I talked to my mother for about half an hour and I told her I was going to see my husband. She said "Does he know you're coming? I said "No, I just need to see him." I ran upstairs to my house and I got in the shower. I needed to relax for just a moment, I did not have to work this weekend and I didn't know the next time I would have another weekend off; especially now that I was changing shift, so I needed to see him. I did not make any reservation with Rosemary so and I did not want to drive so I knew I had to catch that Prison Gap Bus.

I got my LV duffle bag out of the closet and I put my long Ashley Stewart Jean dress in it with my red riding boots, my under garments, my jewelry, my Blue Jean Versace perfume, my makeup bag and my 3/4 red Via Accenti heavy suede coat with the lamb skin; all nicely folded in the LV bag. Then I headed for my journey. I got in my truck and I drove it to 59th Street and parked it in an overnight parking lot nearby where the Prison Gap bus pick-up was. I walked to the Prison Gap bus and waited to board the bus.

I boarded the bus. I was so tired but there was some one that was on the bus that I noticed. She was a young girl; very pretty and she was very dark skinned. Her skin was smooth like a baby. She had been singing this Patti Labelle song and I heard her reach the note like it was so simple. I could not believe that I was hearing this, it was like as soon as I found something I was interested in GOD was giving me more ambition. I don't know what it was but I would never hear anyone sing on this bus. There is usually women that are arguing or literally fighting on the bus. So as I pass her, I went to sit in the back of the bus but I continued to listen; it was smooth, it was right; I just listened and went to sleep. I got up when the bus driver said we will be at Greenhaven in 40 minutes please get your things together for you departure.

Chapter XIX

The Discovery of Janette (R&B Artist)

I started to get my things together to get off the bus, as I passed her I said "You have a great singing voice." She said "Thank you." I said "You are welcome." It was time to get off the bus and onto my visit. As I got off the bus I saw that the young lady was getting off too so I said "Who are you visiting?" and she said my boyfriend." I then knew that she was very young. I said "What is your name?" She said "Janette." I said "That is a pretty name." She said "What is your name?" I said "Rafaela." She said "That is pretty and it is different." I said "Thank you Janette, keep the music in your mouth, it may do you good one day." She said "Thank you and enjoy your visit." I said "Thank you."

I went into the door and as I registered and waited for the C.O. to check me in. Then, while I waited for C.O. to approve my visit, I continues to talk to Janette. I found out a lot more about Janette and I said well Janette, it was good talking to you. If you ever decide that you want to pursue your sing career, call me; and I handed her my business card. Before anything else was said the C.O. called my name for me to go through the gate and enter the visiting room. I went in and sat in the designated seat that was given to me by the C.O. and I waited for Antoine. Antoine came out for the visit and my world was new, I was so ready to see my husband and to just kiss him and sit by him. I was so happy and he was happy to see me.

Antoine said "Ok Mrs. Barbour, what has been happening? How is T.J? How is the business doing?"

I said "Well Mr. Barbour, if you would go one question at a time I could probably answer them." Antoine said "Ok" I said "The business is doing well, TJ is fine and all things are coming around." I discussed with him that TJ is working hard on his first track and that he continues to write songs. He did get his picture taken and Veronica is working on his resume. It's all good. Antoine then asked about how I was doing with work and if I was enjoying what I am doing with the business. I said "Yes." Antoine said "I wish I was with you. I said I would keep you with me always. Well, when you get his tape complete please send me one." I said "Of course." Then we decided to go get some chicken wings from the vending machine. As I walked to the vending machine with Antoine Janette started to point her finger at me; showing her boyfriend who she was talking to on the bus. Antoine said "Why is that girl pointing her finger at you?" I said "Because we were talking on the bus. She is a very good singer so I gave her my card." Antoine smiled and said "Well you are on your game" I looked at Antoine and said "No, I am a business woman with a business and I have to keep my ears open and ready for success!"

I continue to go with Antoine to get the wings, french fries and Nestea in a can. Then we returned to our seats. We continue to talk this time about his business and when I would have to go back to the Dominicans for a pick-up. I would have to take it uptown to someone by the name of Rahmeen. I did not know him but it was ok because I knew that I would be safe Antoine always made sure that the people he had dealings with would never hurt me. Antoine was a beast. I agreed, we kissed and of course Antoine wanted to touch his wife but I kept saying no; so this was one time that he agreed. We talked about Mommy. Antoine was always concerned with his mother-in-law so after the conversation about Mommy, Antoine and I got hungry. We went to put the wings in the microwave. It was always a snuggling session near the microwave because other people were always near the microwave and they would block the C.O. so he could not see and that's when I would always have my fun. I guess the sneaking to get a feel was the exciting part about that situation.

We snuggled until the microwave stopped; I was of course, all hot and bothered and Antoine was hard as a stick. But then we had to control ourselves and wait a minute before pulling the food out of the microwave because he had to make sure that "Big Boy " calms down. He could not walk around with a hard on, the C.O. would know. As I took the food out we put the food on the table and went to take pictures while the food cools down. The picture section was known for everyone getting off because it was a place that was also blocked from the C.O.s. If a lot of people were there waiting to take pictures, Antoine and I would take our pictures and then go back to the table to eat.; There was about three hours left to the visit and of course we played our card games, Crazy 8, Spades, and 500 Rummie. After playing our games we spoke about one visit a month. I would come the first week of next month, which would be February. Antoine agreed and we kissed some more and played around a little, then the C.O. said it was time. I looked at Antoine and said "Ok Papi, I will see you in two weeks." and He said "Ok Mommy, love you." I said "I love you too." I got up and left. I left the visiting floor and I waited outside for the bus. As I waited, Janette came over and said "Rafaela, you and your husband make a nice couple and you and him have so much fun when you see each other." I looked at her and said "We have an understanding." Janette then said "I would like to talk to you sometime." I said "Ok, when you are ready just call me." Janette said "I am going to call you Friday." I said "Ok." and then I got on the bus and she went to her seat.

As I sat in my seat I just continue to reminisce about the visit with Antoine. It was something I needed. As I dozed off it was time to get off of the bus and get my car out of the overnight garage. I drove home. It was two weeks before going to the next visit.

Chapter XX

Reconnecting with Janette (R&B Artist)

Friday night at 9:30pm, I packed my brown Ellen Tracy velour sweatsuit, with my Coach sneakers into my Coach back pack with all the undergarments inside, including all my jewelry and White Diamond perfume. I drove back to Brooklyn to my best friend Rosie's house and I parked my car in front of her house. I jumped on the train to Manhattan; 59th and Columbus Circle. I wanted to see my husband up at Greenhaven Correctional. It had been about a month that I had not been up to visit. I was just overwhelmed with all the businesses. The new artist TJ, on the "Management label." My job "Sanitation" and then checking up on my unlicensed pharmaceutical business.

I just took a chance on the Prison Gap bus. I prayed that it was not crowded and that they would not ask me if I made a reservation. I got to the bus and I waited until they called for Greenhaven Correctional and I just got on the bus.

The bus driver was calling names and then he said "Who are you going to see?" I told him my husband's name and his inmate number, the driver said "Ok, I see you did not make a reservation." I said "I did, but I have no number. When I called the lady took my information and just hung up. She did not give me a seat number." He said "Ok, I will tell her not to forget names." I said "Thanks".

I sat next to this young girl, she was just singing her heart out and I was just listening. I did not say anything the whole ride. She was singing and she sounded very good but I just kept my mouth shut. She was a very young, tall Black girl with pretty skin. She was heavy busted and she sounded like Patti Labelle; she had a tone of a high pitch soprano voice. I was amazed at her voice; it was so beautiful it put me to sleep in such comfort.

I got up as the driver said Greenhaven, I notice that she got up too so I said "Are you going to visit someone in Greenhaven?" she said "Yes, I'm going to visit my boyfriend." I said "You have a beautiful voice." She said "Thank you." Do you sing anywhere? She said "I sing in church, I do background for some people." I said "Ok, I am a Manager at Barbour Entertainment Company.

Do you have management? She said "No." I said "I am Rafaela and I gave her my card." As I was going into the building she said my name is Janette. I remember you from a few months ago. I was talking to you on the bus, it a pleasure meeting you. She asked "After the visit, can we talk?" I said "Yes."

I went on to my visit, going through the usual; going to the correction officer, filing the paper, waiting to be searched and then getting the approval for my visit with my husband. I got into the visiting room and I waited.

Antoine entered the room and I was excited. I was always excited to see him. He was my Knight in Shining Armor; he was my other half, my soul mate. We just had so much of the same qualities it was not funny. I was so happy to see him. It was like being in another world when

I went to see him, even though it was prison; it was like wonderland for me.

Antoine came in; I just jumped on him and I kissed him. He said "Mommy, are you alright?" I said "Yes, just happy to see you." Antoine said "Ok, is there something you want to tell me?" I said "Like what?" He said "Did you do something wrong?" I said "No Baby, it has just been a long week. He said "So what happened, the business has you drained?" I said "Yes, but I can handle it."

I wish you were home working it with me. Antoine said "I know but you are doing a great job." I said "Thanks." He asked how is working with TJ. I said good, he is doing his track now and it's almost complete. Antoine said "All three?" I said "No, we finally have one complete and working on the second." He said "That's good, when it's finished could you sent me a copy?" I said "Sure, I don't see why not Mr. Vice President of Barbour Entertainment." Antoine just laughed and we continue to talk about the other business in the street. I always kept him aware of everything. Antoine said "So how about your new artist Janetta?" I said "She did not sign a contract. We have a meeting this week on Wednesday." He said "GOOD!" We continued to do our usual, go to the Food Vendors and then warm the food up and take our picture. Pictures were always the best part of the visit. We would always find a way to indulge in our sexual desires, near the picture line, it always stay crowded so the C.O. could never see what people were doing. I personally stopped feeling bad about sexual indulgence in the visiting room because he was my husband.

I never thought of the respect factor because we were so discrete; no one ever saw us, after that of course we went to play cards and for some reason Antoine always won. It was because by then I would be in the daze of our sexual experience that had just taken place. After the game it was almost time for the visit to be over and I said to my husband "I will be very busy this week and for a few more weekends." So Antoine said "I know that you are building this business so if I could see you once a month that would be good." and I agreed. I also told him that I will be meeting with the Accountant.

Antoine said "You must be coming off" I look at him and said "Don't worry just keep your money coming." We laughed and then the C.O. said that it was about 30 minutes before end of visit. We talked about the experienced that we had encountered and smiles. I kissed him and I left. Antoine said" Mommy, I'll call you tonight about 10.00pm." I said "Ok." Then I left the visit.

Janette came over to me and said "Mrs. Barbour could we meet for you to explain that contract?" I said "Sure." I gave her an appointment for Wednesday about 3:00pm; just as I had told Antoine. We got on the bus and Janette continued to talk about her singing expertise and what she wanted to do. I continued to listen and I gave her my expectations of what I wanted as an artist signed under my management agreement.

The more we talked the closer we got to the City. As we continued to get more intense in the conversation it was time to go. We were back at 59th street. I told Janette "I will see you Wednesday about 3:00pm in my office. The address was 700 Victory Blvd., Staten Island, NY, Suite 4a." She agreed and we went our separate ways. It was the hustle and bustle out of the City to my house but I had to go to Rosie's house to pick my vehicle up then drive home.

It was 10:00pm when my cell phone rang. I knew it was Antoine 'cause I had forward my house calls to the cell.

I said "Yes Baby?" He said "Where are you?" I said "Just getting in my car at Rosie's house. He said "Tell Rosie I said hello." I said "I did not stop in because I have to go to work at 12:00am. You forgot I am grave yard shift, 12:00 am starting Monday morning." He said "Yes I forgot, but I'll call you when you get off." I said "Ok, Love you." I drove to Staten Island and got in the shower very quickly and got in my uniform and went to work for 12:00 roll call.

I got to work and I did relay all night. I did not have the strength to do garbage so I just dumped the truck. It was called relays because you go back and forth to the Arthur Kill dump and then back to the garage. I had to do 6 relays a night. After the 6 relays, I handed my supervisor the dump tickets and I went home. Thank GOD for working across the street from home. I got right in the bed and I slept. The phone rung about 8:00am am I said "Hello." It was my supervisor Mike; he said "Are you coming to sign out?" I said "Yes Mike, thank you. I will be there in a few." He said "Ok Rafaela." I got up in my pajamas and I went to sign out, then came home and got back in the bed.

It was around 12:00pm and Antoine called; we talked for a little while and I had to get prepared to go to the studio to check on TJ. I had him in a studio in East New York so I was going to see if he had completed his second track. I went to the studio and TJ had not yet completed the second track but I understood that a good track takes time to complete. With the engineer and the artist it would come together so I just stayed until it was complete and took TJ home. As we were driving, TJ and I got to talking about life in general and that was the first time that TJ had asked me something so personal that I know I could not tell my husband. I did not need Antoine to be putting out a hit on anyone. TJ had asked me if I ever got lonely being in this industry without my husband. I responded "Yes, but it's not that easy; I keep my head on business." TJ then said "You are very attractive and sometimes I think of you." I looked at TJ and I said "TJ your wife loves you and I love my husband so let's just keep this professional." He said "No, I understand "But," I said "TJ there is no BUT." We had arrived at his house and I say "Good night TJ." I drove off and went to my house on Staten Island; we never visited that conversation again.

Chapter XXI

Samuel Signing on to Barbour Entertainment

It was the beginning of March, and I had two Artists under the management company. I was going to meet TJ and Janette at the studio in Manhattan so I decide to take the Staten Island Ferry across to Manhattan. I did not want to be in traffic or the hustle and the bustle of finding parking in the lower part of Manhattan so I took the ferry across and enjoyed my scenery.

I got off the ferry; I was walking to the N train towards Wall Street and I was thinking of the people that I have been blessed to do business with and all the opportunities that where opening up for "BBE" (Barbour Entertainment).

I walked down a little past Wall Street and as walked I continued to hear this voice that was so amazing to my ears. It was like Luther was playing on a radio in front of me but I just could not see Who or Whom had the radio.

I walked faster to try to find the radio that was playing and it was a young Spanish boy about 16 years of age, very handsome, that was singing.

I stopped him and asked him "Do you sing for a church or a band?" He said "No, I just left the Staten Island Ferry, my friend and I always sing for money." I said "You are kidding me?" He said "No." I then asked him his name and he said "Samuel." I said "I'm Rafaela with Barbour Entertainment." He said "Hello." I said "Do you like singing or is it just a hobby?"

Samuel said "I love to sing but my mother is not able to afford for me to go to singing school or any other program that would help me achieve my goals or dreams. She has had it very difficult the last couple of years with her and my dad are divorcing."

I said "Samuel, it could be your luck day. I am a manager for a company "BBE" (Barbour Entertainment) and I am looking for a male singer. I have a female singer and a great rap artist so I will give you my card." As I handed Samuel my card he looked at me as though in disbelief that this was happening to him. He then gave me his home number; he did not have a cell phone. I want you to call me, but first talk it over with your mother than have her call me. As I continue down to the studio I was in deep thought about how so many people were going through things and that they could not assist their children with their dreams and needs. I felt as though GOD has given me this time to help others in need.

As I got to the studio Janette and TJ were outside. They could not get inside the studio because the Conductor (engineer) was not there yet; so we went to the corner to have something to eat until the time had arrived for the session.

As we were in the studio laying the tracks, TJ was writing the words to this collaboration. I keep thinking of Samuel and so I mention him to the other two artists that where under my management. They where so happy that they kept continuously asking "Are you going to sign him?" and I say "I don't know, it would be up to him and his mother, he is very young." We had finished the session about 6:00pm and it was time to leave the studio. We parted and went our separate ways until the next studio session.

A few days went by and I had not heard from Samuel so I decide to call the number that he had given me. A woman said "Hello." I said "Hello, may I speak to Samuel?" She said "Whom shall I say is calling?" I said "Rafaela from BBE." That is when the women said "Hello Rafaela, this is Sammy's mother Martina." I said "Hello Mrs. Martina." Martina then said "So you are the women that Samuel met a couple of days ago?" I said "Yes Mrs. Martina." then she said "Why don't we meet up at my house next week some time, there are some things that I would like to discuss with you." I said "Ok Mrs. Martina." She said "No Rafaela, call me Martina." I said "Very well." She then said bye to me and put Sammy on the phone. Sammy said "Hello Mrs. Rafaela, how are you?" I said I was fine, Sammy then said "I'm glad you got to speak to my mother and that you are going to meet with her next week." I said "I will, I'm glad you spoke to her about me Sammy and you did not have disbelief." Sammy then said "No, all I have is faith." I talked to him a bit more then our phone conversation was over and I had given him the date to give his mother. I had to check my schedule while on the phone so it was a go for Thursday of the next week.

The week had come for me to meet with Samuel's mother Mrs. Martina. They lived in the Projects in Manhattan; right off of the FDR. They were called the Baruch Houses. So I parked my truck on the side of the FDR and I went to 711 FDR Drive and went to the 4 the floor, Apt. 4D.

It was going to be my first meeting talking to a parent about their child signing a contract to a management company. I was not a child but I was only in my thirties and I just felt, that it would have been a hard thing to do asking another parent to trust in me because I looked so young. They would never believe that I was as old as I was. I went in there with so much confidence that I had won over Samuel's mother and she had given me her blessing. They signed the contract on my terms. It was another VICTORY MOMENT! I had the greatest team in the world.

Chapter XXII

The Accountant

It was the end of March 1996 when I had finally made an appointment with an Accountant. It was one that I picked out of the Yellow Pages and that the business bureau had on their roster for good business. The accountant's office was on Morningstar Road in Staten Island, NY. The office looked like it was under some major construction. It was kind of frightening to me being that I expected an accounting office to be more office structured.

I looked around and my inner spirit said to continue to attempt doing business in this place. I have always listened to my gut feeling on the inner side of my soul. The lady at the desk, by the name of Lily, said to me "Can I help you?" I said "I am Rafaela Barbour and I have an appointment with Gregory Carpenter." She said "Okay." She went in the back office and told him I was there. Mr. Gregory Carpenter came out.

He was tall and he was very handsome but I could tell that he had been going through a change in his life. Gregory walked up to me and shook my hand. He said "What can I do for you little lady?" I said "Well, I spoke to you on the telephone and I have a small business." and Gregory said "Oh, you're the young lady I talked to with the entertainment business; that is the "First Sanitation Woman" in Staten Island, yes?"

Rafaela come to the back with me; that is where his office was.

I walked into the back office and sat down to discuss the business. I sat down in the back office and the first thing that came out of Mr.C mouth was, "How do you pick up garbage with those nails? How is it being the first women in Staten Island with all those men?"

I looked at Mr. C and said "Very easy, I grab the garbage bag with my fingers not my nails and throw them in the harper; that was the term used in the department for the back of the garbage truck.

Mr. C then asked, "How do they treat you being a woman?" They respect me. I am like one of the boys to them. We have a good relationship on the job. Mr.C laughed and said "Ok garbage woman, talk to me about your business."

I have three artists on contract under my Management company Barbour Entertainment and one is going into a showcase for 5,000.00, in Atlanta. It is called "FreakNic." As his manager, I would be getting a percentage of money in whatever he does in the industry; Whether its rap, dance, movies, etc. Mr. C, if he wins then he will be getting a recording contract too with Sony, Columbia, or Warner Brothers. I have to be very prepared for what is to come. I always think long-term so I need to put money in place in order to be clear and comfortable in my everyday spending.

I have been putting him in different shows and most of them are for money so I need you to see help me in banking and get a heads up on what a possible good investment may be without spending all of my funds.

Mr. C said "How much money did you put into the business?"

I said "A couple thousands." Mr. C said "Do you know how much exactly? I said "No, that's why I am here."

I handed him a big folder of all the receipts that I had from the time that I had started the business.

Mr. C looked at me and said "Well Little Lady, you sure know how to keep things in order." As we talked about everything that was purchased and every event that was covered, Mr. C said to me "You sure spend a lot of money and you don't think about the cost." I said "No, I have it to cover."

Mr. C said, "Well little lady, I will get all this stuff you brought to me in order and I will give you a call." I said "Thanks Mr. C." He said "Call me Gregory." I said "Fine then, Gregory I will see you when you set up ann appointment to discuss my situation." He said "Well tell Lily to give you and appointment for next week." I said "Ok, thank you."

As I walk out I notice a look on Gregory's face. It was a look as to say, WOW! That young black woman got her stuff in order and her vision was long term. I believe that's why he continued to work with me. The following week I went to Mr. C's office. I had my Corporation book, stamp, and seal. This was so that I could get a corporate account at the bank.

Mr. C taught me the difference between corporate and non-corporate, Inc., and all other stuff pertaining to business.

Mr. C taught me my do's and my don'ts of how to spend my money. We talked and had a drink on our new business venture. I would have to come every three months to check up and make sure that I was carrying my business in a professional matter.

Chapter XXIII

The Trying Time of Loneliness

The following weeks I decide to take my business to another level. I started to attend "Open Mics". These are little events in the clubs where you can find new talent. It was like "Spoken Word" but instead of with poetry it focused on musical artists. I started networking for a couple of weeks and attended everything that the big City of New York was offering with the talent shows. I started to introduce myself to other people in the music industry, but something was missing in my life and that was my other half. I was getting lonely so I decided to go and see him on the next weekend.

It was now May of 1996; I hadn't seen my husband so I need to rejuvenate. I needed to speak to my husband so I drove up to see him. I went to see him because I had missed him and besides he was my comforter. I needed to hold on to my other half; being in the world without your loved one as a woman can be very testie; if that is even a word, but I wanted to discuss with him my new business venture. Nevertheless, I just wanted to get all that I could, up in his face, some kisses, some hugs, and some feels; whatever we could do, I wanted to do it. I had really missed my husband and he kept me going. A dose of Antoine and I was good!

So as I drove up to the Greenhaven Facility I noticed that there was always a dark shadow over the prison; something that my mother had describe to me. I could never figure that out. It was one of the cloudiest prisons ever. I filled the registration form out and I waited to see my husband. I was getting more and more excited. As he came towards me I just smiled and jumped on him as though I had never seen him before. It was my anxiety; Antoine looked at me and said "What is this about?" Is there something that you need to tell me?" Every time that I was over excited to see Antoine the first thing he would say is 'What is this about?' So I said "Baby you have no idea that I just miss you and I need you out in the street with me." Antoine looked at me and asked the question "Is it too much?" I said "No, it's just that sometime I miss my mans' touch." Antoine then looked at me and said "Is there someone that you are...." before he could finish the sentence I said "No, there you go, I just wish that you were doing this with me." When that happened, Antoine did not want to sit down.

He did not want to sit down so we decided to go to the vending machine to get the basic food that we ate out of the machine. 6 packs of hot wings, 2 packs of french fries, 2 fish sandwiches, 2 Snickers bars, 2 waters and 2 sodas. This was our usual; after getting our food we decide to go outside. It was getting warm and we wanted to spend our visit outside. We got to the table that the Correction Officer had assigned us on the outside, we put our food down, and Antoine says "let's talk while we walk." I said "Ok." It was not like we were going to take a long walk; it was confined. Greenhaven had an outside visiting room that was about 2600 feet by 3600 feet and it was in a square, so we walked the square.

Antoine said "I want to talk to you Fita." I said "Ok speak." Antoine said "I know that I am your husband and you are my wife and I know that you are faithful to me; but I want you to know that if you ever have a desire to see or be with another man I would suggest that you be with Tom, Dick, Bill, Bob and Harry." I look at him and said "Why would you want me to be with so many men?" Antoine looked in my eyes and said "If you were to be with different men you would never get to love them as you do me, but if you allow yourself to get involved with one man, if you started to be with just one man, that is where you will build a relationship." I looked at Antoine and said "Thank you, but no thanks. I appreciate that you understand, you are a bigger man to tell your wife that, but no thanks!"

As we continue to walk around I said "I thank you for just understanding that I get lonely, but it's not about sleeping with other people. It about living life itself." Antoine looked at me and said "I know that this is not what you signed up for when you were growing up but we are here." I just looked at him and I kissed him as the tears rolled down my eyes and I said "I know that I said "I DO" and that is all I know."

Antoine and I walked back to our seated tables and we played some cards and we just hugged one another. It was about 1:00pm when we decide to warm up the food so we walked inside and put the food in the microwave. We ate and it was about 40 minutes before visitation was over. We just kissed and hugged each other until it was time. It was now three o'clock and we had not talked about the business so I know Antoine would be calling during the week to discuss business. It was Sunday and I know that it was a long week ahead of me so I just said good bye and I never turned around. I walked off the visiting floor and walked out of the correctional facility. I got to the parking lot and got in my car. As I started to drive I could not get the thought out of my head about if I got lonely. It was something that I didn't understand for the life of me. Antoine, the one that will kill for me, is saying that it is ok to have someone else. I continue to drive and I stopped in PA (Pennsylvania) for gas. Then I continue to drive home. It was now 6:30pm and I was getting close to home. I got a call on my cell about a networking party that was going to be coming up so I knew that I needed to be there. I will put it on my calendar when I got home so that I would not schedule anything for that day. It was coming up for the next weekend. As I walked into the house I wrote it on my calendar, I took a shower and laid down because I know that I would be going in at 12:00am.

It was 11:00pm by the time I woke up, I got dressed and it was time to go to work after that long trip. I walked around the corner to my job, it was roll call. I got my ticket from the Garage Supervisor and went to the dump with my first truck. After that, I continue to dump trucks; the quota was 6 trucks a shift, after the sixth truck it was usually about 5:00am. I was finished and there was still three hours left before the shift was over. I would go home and sleep until 8:00am and then come back to the job and sign out.

It was 8:20am, the phone rang I said "Hello" and it was my supervisor Melvin, he said "Are you planning on signing out?" I said "Yes Mel, what time is it?" He said "It is after 8:00." I said "Ok, I will be right there."

My supervisors were so cool about me going home as long as they could reach me in an emergency. The supervisor did not mind me leaving the garage, hey; I was the only woman Sanitation worker on Staten Island so they did not mind. My locker room was on the other side of the garage and they knew I did not want to be over on the other side by myself so it was ok for me to go home. I put my sweats on and went across the street to sign-out and came back to my house to sleep.

Chapter XXIV

Preparation for the Extravaganza

I woke up about 1:00pm and I went to the telephone to call my mother at work; just to say hello because I was not up when she left to go to work. My mother lived downstairs and I live upstairs. We had a two family house in Staten Island. I spoke to her she said that she was going to her girlfriend's house and she would have them drop her off at home later. She did not want me to worry about her not coming home her usual time. I said "Ok." and I hung up.

I went to the kitchen to fix me some breakfast as the telephone rang; it was the man of my dreams, my husband Antoine. Antoine said "Good morning Mrs. Barbour." I said "Good morning Mr. Barbour." "How was your night at work?" he asked. I said "It was good, thank you." I then asked him how he slept without me. He said "I didn't." I said "So you mean to tell me that you have been up all this time?" He said "I never really sleep without you." I say "So how are you managing these days and years?" He said "I have you next to me in the bed." I just laughed and said "You have a picture on the bed?" Uh." He said "Yes." I said "Good job my dearest husband."

I continue to cook my breakfast. I spoke to my husband about all that was going to take place in the next few weeks. I was not going to visit; I would have to focus on the business, the events that I was going to have, and the introduction of "The Artists Of Barbour Entertainment". I was going to be at a very big club and with the advertisement and tickets there was just so much that I had to keep up with. I had to have everything in place so I wanted him to understand that it was a lot for me to take control of these things that had to be done; and still come to visit him.

Antoine said "Its fine, do what you have to do and I will still send you your money." I said "Thank you." We continue to talk about the event that I was going to. It was networking for the business and I told him that I was looking forward to meeting a lot of people that are in the management business or have CEO status. Antoine said "That is good, that's the people you need to meet." I said "Yes Baby, but you know that I have to get my gear (clothes) right." Antoine just laughed and said "That is just an excuse for you to go shopping because you have hundreds of clothes in your closet." I said "You may be right but you know the "DIVA" must get something different." Antoine giggled and said "Ok, so I assume that today is your shopping day." I said "You are correct!"Antoine said "Ok Mrs. Barbour, I will let you go so that you could get a fabulous dress or jumpsuit for the event. I will call you later, Love you." I said the same and hung up.

It was now time to get in the shower and get dressed because I needed to go shopping. It was Monday morning and the event was the same evening. I had my chart day (day off) for Tuesday which meant that I did not have to go to work this Monday night. I got out of the shower and I put my brown Phat Farm sweatsuit on and my Gucci sneakers, I got my Gucci bag and ran downstairs to the car. I got into the car and I drove to the Staten Island Mall.

It was about 3:30pm when I arrived to the mall. I went to Macy's and they did not have anything I wanted. I went to a couple more stores but of course I did not find anything that I wanted to wear. I just went on across the Bayonne Bridge (New Jersey) and went to New Jersey to the Nordstrom store; I knew that I would find something there.

As I got into Nordstrom's I saw a black and purple Gaultier jumpsuit. It was like Bermuda shorts. I just had to have it, it was slinky and it dropped down on your curves, I took it off the rack and I went into the shoe department to look for some purple high heel boots. I was looking for one that was open-toe like a sandal. It was June and it was very warm out. I wanted to look like a Goddess. I continue to look for the sandals and of course I found the perfect one. It was open-toe, it had straps all the way across the front and it went as high as my knees. They were made by Moschino. I pick those sandals and I went to the register to pay. It was now about 5:45 or 6:00pm. I still had to go to Brooklyn to get my nails done. It was a must and I was pressed for time. I know that the nail salon closes at 8:00pm so I had about an hour to get into the nail salon. I drove out of the Nordstrom mall and headed to the New Jersey Turnpike so I could take the Holland Tunnel to the Brooklyn Bridge. I would get off on Flatbush Avenue and go to Bridge Street and get into the salon on time.

Elaine was always there waiting. She was my Nail Technician. I got in there and Elaine was busy so I was hoping she would take me next, it was about 8:25pm when Elaine was finished with my nails. I paid her and then I thanked her and left. It was now 8:30pm when I left the salon and I went to the BQE toward the Verrazano Bridge to go home to Staten Island. I got home about 9:20pm and I got into the tub. I just needed to sit and take it all in. I had covered everything that I needed to do so I just sat in the tub for about 20 minutes and then I got up, turned the shower on, and I had a lot of time to get to the Networking Event. It did not start until 11:00pm. It was 10:30pm and I was getting ready for the event when the phone rang. It was the correction facility Operator. "Would you accept a collect call from Antoine Barbour?" I accepted it and I said "Hello Mr. B." And he said "Hey there Mrs. B., what is going on?" I said "I am getting ready for the event" and Antoine said "So what are you wearing?" I said "A short jump suit." Antoine said "How short?" I said "To the knee." Antoine said "What are you showing?" I said "Nothing." Antoine said "How does it fit?" I said "Slinky and it clings to my body." He said "Very tempting." I said "My husband is the only man that can touch." Antoine said "GOOD JOB Mrs. B., so you are going to knock then?" I said "I will try, Baby I don't want to get there too late; it's not good for business." He said "You are right so I will hang up. I love you and I'll call you tomorrow." I said "I love you too." I continue to get dressed and I put on my Victoria Secret body lotion and then I put on my Victoria fragrance. I put my makeup on my face, put on the slinky jump suit and I put my hair up in a french bun. I got all of my stuff packed into my purple Fendi clutch and put my purple Moschino strapped sandal on that went up to my knees. I look fabulous; just like a Goddess. I walked downstairs and went to my mother's house to say hello and to get her approval on what I was wearing. My mother said "Wow, you looking like a Stunning Goddess I say "Thanks Mommy. I will be coming in late. I have an event." My mother said "Ok have fun and go get that contract Mrs. B." I said "Thanks Mommy, I love you. See you tomorrow." I left my mother's house and I got into the car and drove to Manhattan. The event was on 38th Street between 5th and 6th Avenues. It was a place called The Monument.

Chapter XXV

April 1996 - Meeting Hassan, Promoter of Uptown Marketing

As I walk into the party that Uptown Marketing was giving; all eyes were on me. It was good to make such an impact on people and it represents the company Barbour Entertainment that I worked for; let alone owned. This marketing company was a company known to promote your business to the new world of Music. They would give you a lot of exposure and that's what I needed.

This young man came over to me and said "Hello I am Hassan." and I said "Hello, how are you?" He said, "I am well and yourself?" I said "I am fine." He said "I can see that you are fine, but I did not ask you how you look I asked you how you feel." I looked at him and smiled then I said "Thank you, I feel great."

Hassan then said "So, what brings you here to this lovely event?" I said "Well I'm Rafaela Barbour, CEO of Barbour Entertainment. I have three artists and I'm just looking for some exposure for them and possibly recording contracts for them as well."

Hassan said "I'm the Vice President of Uptown Marketing. Hassan said "Tell me about your company and your artists?" I continue to talk and give him a brief introduction of my company and told him what my goals are within the next few months. He was very impressed and said he needed to introduce me to the CEO & President of Uptown Marketing Inc. We continue to talk and walk closer to the bar where a young man was seated with a glass of Hennessey.

Hassan said "Rafaela this is Gerral, and Gerral this is Rafaela from Barbour Entertainment." Gerral said "Ms. or Mrs. Rafaela?" I said "Mrs." Gerral then said How could I be of assistance to you?" I then said "Well, I was looking to do a lot of business and I need to hire a Marketing and Promotion company for the next few weeks. I will be doing some very important events and I need the best of the best on my team."

I am going to do my First Annual "70's Players' Ball" with Hot 97 and WBLS on September 30th. The DJ is Red Alert and the host is Bugsy from Hot 97. I also have Ralph McDaniel to cover it on Video Music Box. I need the best promotion team and I need them to be concentrated on my business. There will be a lot of other events that I will be doing before the end of the year.

Mr. Gerral said "Ok then Mrs. Rafaela; I would like to meet with you on Tuesday in my office about 2:00pm." I agreed and of course we shook hands. I continued to network with the other producers, agents and Artist representatives; also some of the Sony label employees. It was about an hour that I was there and then they had a showcase of new artists. I stood there with one of the Engineers from Track Masters and Hassan came over to me. He said "You may want to listen to this young man, he is at all the showcases and I don't believe he has a manager." I said "Thanks Hassan, I will listen to him." When they introduced the act it was a young man from Queens aka "DJ" I had already had a "TJ" on my roster. It was wonderful just listening to him rhyme. I could not believe it, he was very GOOD, just like my TJ but in a different matter. I waited until the young man finished and I approached him. I said "I am Rafaela from BBE (Barbour Ent.), that was very good. So how often do you come to showcases?" DJ said "I come a lot." I said "Do you have a manager?" DJ said "I don't." I said "Well look, I know that you may want to consider a manager in the long run so here is my card. Call me when you want to talk." I hand him my card and I went off with Junie from Chung King Studio.

The evening was great! I had really put it down with my networking game. I had networked with so many labels that I could just send my press kit to them directly.

It was the end of the evening for me; it was about 3:00am. I was on my way home when I heard a young man's voice from behind me say, "Really looking good in that jumpsuit Mrs. B." I said "Thanks." and continued to walk. The voice said "So, are you married?" I said "Yes." He said "So why are you out alone?" I then turned around and notice that it was Keith, an A&R (Artist representative) for Def Jam that was interested in me but I just wanted to sign my artist TJ. I said "Keith, what do you want?" He said "You." I said "Keith, I am a business woman and I am not in this business to mess with men. I'm here to work and run a business." He then said "I would like to give TJ a recording contract if you meet with me a 12:00am at my house." I looked at Keith and in a very angry voice I said "I'm not looking for a deal for myself. I am negotiating a deal for my artist. Keith, what would I look like coming to your house at midnight? And then, you open the door with you boxer shorts open and say oops... excuse me. I believe if you want to sign TJ on a recording contract through Def Jam Entertainment then we could meet in your office."

I continued to walk to my car got inside, and drove off thinking... it was just so crazy how the men in the industry thought that they could just sleep around with women and make it a fair exchange. But I was not going to be uses or bought. I was in this for business purposes only and I did not need a man; I had a husband for that. I was fine with going to see him every week; kissing, flirting and being touched by my husband. With all the thoughts in my head, I realized that I had already reached home and I was parking. As I was getting out of the car in front of my house the phone rang and that voice haunted me again. I said it would be good for us to get together in his office soon. I said, if it is for business, yes. Keith, if it is for you desires and lust NO!!! I hung up and went into the house, got into the shower, put my pj's and went to sleep.

Chapter XXVI

Doing Business with Uptown Marketing (Promotion Team)

It was now Tuesday, early afternoon and I had an appointment with Gerral, the CEO of Uptown Marketing at 2:00pm. I put on my red dress by Estee Lauder and a pair of natural sheer stockings with my red Nina Ricci pump. I put everything that I needed in my Louie bag; from my business cards to my makeup, money, and my phone. I started out a little late so I was just trying to make up time because I did not want to be late. That is not how I do business. All of my life I've been an on-time person and I could not ruin that.

I got in the car and headed for Manhattan to the office. It was located at 147 E 48th Street between 5th and 6th Avenue. It was a very elegant building. I took the elevator to the 10th floor and as I got out of the elevator, Hassan was there to greet me.

"Good afternoon Mrs. B.". I said "Good afternoon Hassan." He then took me to an office; it was laid out very nice; everyone's office was different in this company. It was very impressive in this marketing company. I walk into Mr. Gerral's office and we got right to business.

I told him my vision and I told him the budget. Mr. Gerral agreed to all of my terms and I was done. We shook hands and I was on my way to the studio to see about TJ, Samuel and Janette.

It was going to be a good event and my artists were going to be very prepared. I walked out of the office and into Hassan's office. I said "Hassan, I will update you on the details by phone and I will have my secretary write up the contract and fax it over to you." Mr. Gerral and Hassan said "Good." then, "Mrs. B., can I walk you to the door?" I said "Yes."

It was 3:30pm and I needed to be at the studio by 4:30pm and out of the studio but 6pm. I had to get to my house and in bed by 7:30pm so that I could get some sleep before my shift at work. I got to the studio at 4:15pm and I noticed that Samuel was not there. I called his house his mother said he left and should be getting their soon. TJ and Janette were going over their tracks. Janette sounded more and more like Patti Labelle; I started to tear, but I knew that I could not market her in the industry that way. Patti was not going anywhere and there would be no room for Janette, so I asked the producer, "Conductor" what he came up with for collaboration for the three of them. He gave me this track that was on fire! It was special for all three of my artists. Jannette was of course singing on the hook (chorus) and TJ was rapping; and to close it off, Samuel had a voice like Luther and Marvin Gaye (it was a mix of both). When Sammy came in he went straight to the booth and sang his part of the "callabo" the song was done. The song was on FIRE! The name of the song was "Why Should I Love You".

It was done, I had my first callabo, complete to shop for a mix callabo with all of my artists. The timing was good. I scheduled them for studio time for Saturday and I left to make my deadline on getting sleep for work. There was still more time left for them in the studio so I know they would utilize the studio time. Actually, Conductor (engineer) would make sure that they used it well. I got in the car and drove over the Manhattan Bridge to the BQE, over the Verrazano Bridge, down through Bay Street to Victory Avenue. I parked my car, ran in my house, went to the bathroom, jumped in the shower and laid down. I slept until 11:00pm.

Chapter XXVII

Clinton Correctional Facility: First Trailer Visit

September 15, 1996

It was September 15, 1996, a very special day for my husband and I. "First Family Visit" it was a weekend that I could finally get to touch, kiss and make love to my husband without sneaking or Correction Officers telling me what to do. Most people called it "A trailer visit". We both waited over two years for this day. We had applied for this day many of times but were denied because Antoine was always fighting, or not cooperating with the system that he was living under.

I get off the bus and I go into the building as I usually do. I wait for the Correction Officer to call all of the families that are going to have the weekend visit. As I waited to be called I watched how the "COs"(Correction Officers) where checking everything that people were bringing into the trailer visit. You are allowed to bring prepared food; cakes, pies, etc. It was like a privilege for them to give you so much freedom of meals but Correction Officers would dig their hands all in the prepared food to make sure that there was nothing going into the trailer that was not suppose to; I watched them dig into other families cakes and pies before allowing it into the trailer.

Rafaela Barbour was called and as I walk towards the Correction Officer that was going to check my food he asked if there was anything I had that was not allowed to come in. Before he checked I answered no. The Correction Officer proceeded to check my food but I brought canned food and vegetables, lobster, shrimps, steak, and ground beef. That was all my husband wanted. Of course no chicken because that is all we ate on the visiting floor. The C.O. had to dig into my ground beef and the lobster, I had a box of cake mix and frosting that he did not have to open as long as it had the original seal. C.O.s would not open it and I had a few cans of Pepsi and chips.

I then went into another room where they give you an opportunity to pick ten movies so I picked Independence Day, Mobsters Daughter, Bad Boys, The Client, Die Hard, Forrest Gump, and a few others. Then I went into another room and they would check everything else that you had in your suitcase, I was kind of embarrassed because I had all of the edible panties and a lot of sexy lingerie. As for me, I did not want a C.O. to even imagine me in it but the Correction Officer turned around and said "Mrs. Barbour you are going to really turn your husband out!" I said "YES! it has been a long time coming." He just smiled, I was clear to go into the bus that was outside; their where a few other women and children on the bus so I just sat down and waited. There was one more family that had gotten on the bus and the Correction Officer got on the bus and said "Ok, I will be taking you to your trailers for the weekend."

It was so exciting, tears just rolled down my face. The day had finally arrived that I would spend the night and wake up next to Mr. Barbour; after being married to him and spending no more than just five minutes after we got married and 8 hours visits for years. I was really going to spend time with him alone for the first time in three years!

I continue to look out of the window on the bus, looking to see how much further the trailers were from the prison, but then we drove into a wooded area. Finally I saw the gate open and inside the gated area was a community of trailers for the five families that were on the bus along with me. There were two watch towers in the front and the back of the area where Correction Officers were posted to watch the area.

The Correction Officers called all the families by the inmate's name. As I waited for them to call my husband's name I was very amazed that they were just driving families to the entrance of the trailer and leaving. This was surely a privilege because for years it was like being treated like an inmate as well. The Correction Officers where not always nice to people, but I had been blessed because they where always nice to me.

Antoine's name was called and that meant this was my stop. It was my turn to get off the bus and go to the trailer. I walk into the trailer and it was a two bedroom trailer with separate living room, kitchen, and bathroom. It was so big; I could not believe that this was happening. I continue to walk in and I did not know what to do. My husband was not there yet so I decide to unload the suitcase and all the food. I put the food in the refrigerator. I could not believe that there was real silverware (forks, spoon and knives.) I found that strange because they are so strict about everything during the visit that you could not get in if you had a safety pin or tweezers; but the trailers had knives.

This was a real family visit with your loved one. I could not believe that a real knife was available. It really was an honor to have the family visit weekend. I started unpacking my clothes and I heard the door open I said "Antoine", there was no answer and I repeated his name "Antoine", I could not believe that there was no response. All I remember was Antoine kissing my neck and him crying, saying "I can't believe that this is happening after all the trailer visits that I messed up with my bad conduct. I can't believe we are here." I said "Yes, I am finally glad that you started to behave Antoine!" then he took me to the room and he sat me down on the bed. He said "Mommy, I want to apologize for all the trailer visits that where denied." I looked at him and said "What are you talking about Antoine?" then he said "I have been so out of character with my behavior. It took an older man on our visit to help me through this." I said "What do you mean?" He said "Mommy, one of the older inmates took me after one of our visits and sat me down and said to me,"Antoine you have a beautiful wife, look at her, if you don't start to get yourself together to enjoy the privilege that you have here, like family visits, you are going to lose her. Look at your wife, she needs love Antoine." and from that day I started to find a new attitude. We will never ever have anymore trailer visits denied. From that moment we kissed, Antoine undressed me, and he just looked at my body.

I then undressed him and looked at all of those muscles that he had. Antoine lifted me up, spun me around, laid me on the bed and started kissing me all over my body from head to toe. After the kisses where the licks, then the love making. There was no more talking; for three hours, then we got in the shower and my husband made love to me in the shower position were created.

That evening I cooked for my husband for the first time since we had been married. It was also the first time since we were married that we had made love the way a man is supposed to make love to his wife. We watched a few movies and talked about some uplifting things for the future.

Saturday morning came and went with us in bed making love and being adventurous with our bodies. We continued to just explore our bodies and finally we got up and went into the kitchen to cook. I cooked every meal on Saturday so that I would just have to microwave food for the rest of the weekend. I knew that I would not have any more time to cook with the creative weekend and all of this dessert food that I was feeding him and him feeding me. The three years that was backed-up inside of me was now released and I could go on for one year without being backed-up; but once we started to get trailer visits it was one every month.

We were up in the bed, counter top, showers, and living room; you name it, we tried it. It was wonderful and I could not believe that I had been sleeping two nights straight with my husband without being disturbed. Yes, the Correction Officer called every hour to make sure people were still alive, or whatever the purpose was. If you were in the shower and the phone was ringing and you did not pick up the Correction Officer was at your door! Besides that, the trailer visit was great.

It was now Sunday morning and the trailer visit would come to an end at 12:00pm.I started to pack my stuff about 10:00am so that we could still get a little in before departing. I also cleaned the kitchen and put all of the silverware back in place. We made love and at 12:00pm the Correction Officer came to pick Antoine up. The Correction Officer came back for me at 2:00pm and I got back on the bus. The families were picked up separately for security reasons so I was on the bus alone and they escorted me to the gate. I took all my stuff off the bus, went to my car and loaded it up to leave. It must have been about 6:00pm as I was driving home. The phone rang, it was the Correction Department Operator, "Will you accept this call...?" I accept it and it was the man of the hour, Antoine. He said "Mommy" I said "Hey Papi'." He said "How do you feel?" I said "Sore!" He laughed and said "Big Daddy took care of you!" I said "Yes, just what he suppose to do." Antoine laughed and said "I really enjoy my wife." I said "Thanks, I enjoy my husband." He said "How far are you?" I said "I am about 4 hours and 30 minutes away from home so I will get home right after the phones go off. So call me tomorrow. I took the day off." Antoine said "Ok Mommy, I'm going to hang up. I want you to get home safe." I said "Good night Papi."

Chapter XXVIII

APOLLO - 125th Street Ruff, Rugged & Real

Monday, September 18, 1996, I got up in the best mood ever, I had gotten fed by my husband and now it was time to be victorious. It was my last day before going back to work for the week and I wanted to get some things wrapped up and finished.

I knew that there were so many things lined up for me in the next few weeks the trailer visit came at the best time. There were upcoming shows and open mics that my artists were registered to participate in for different prizes, money, and recording contracts. It was going to be a good ending quarter for "BBE", as well as a great beginning quarter for the New Year.

I was getting dressed, the phone rang and I said "Hello." It was Hassan; he said "Mrs. B. how was your weekend?" I said "Great. I spent it with my husband; good quality time." Hassan said "Good he must be a lucky man." I said "I guess he is." Hassan did not know that Antoine was prison; it was not his place to know.

"Hassan, so what up?" Hassan, then said that there was an opportunity for investment on a "big scale show" that I, as well as Barbour Entertainment, could be a part of with

156

some other entertainment company. It would be at the Apollo Theater.

I said "Ok, go on with the numbers (how much does it cost)." Hassan said if you put $3,090 the other two entertainment companies are matching your amount. That will pay for everything; The Apollo, promotion and marketing, radio play, and tickets. We will set it up as an open mic, charging the artists $25.00 to enter with every artist selling ten tickets. It will be open to the public as well. We will have a lot of A&R from every record company there looking for talent, signing right on the spot." I did not even hesitate because the numbers came back when I had calculated them in my brain so I told him to type up the contract and send it to my secretary Tanya. She was the greatest. Anything that was sent to the office, she would contact me right away if I was not there to receive it. She was my back bone and she knew how I felt about business; she would make it happen. She got paid well and on time.

Hassan said "Great Mrs. B. and the other contracts were sent this morning to the office." I said "Thanks." I called the office and I brought Tanya up to speed with the contract that was going to be sent. Tanya was smart, as well as myself, so she said the numbers look right. I said "Thank GOD I have taught her well." I ran the numbers down to Tanya, Tanya then said "same number or more" (meaning number of contracts; if they send more we take it) is what my signature goes on, right Mrs.?" I said "Right." and I hung up.

I figured that I would meet the artists in the studio for the completion of the (A) side of the album (first side). I was shopping them (marketing) as a whole team on Warner Brother recording companies and TJ as a solo artist. Samuel and Jannette was like Peaches and Herb; something that the industry needed and was missing since the 80's. I got to the studio. TJ was not there yet but was on his way. Jannette and Samuel was in the booth laying out the third song and Conductor was "Happier than two pigs in mud." that's what my father use to say when people where happy. It was a joke that I was raised hearing and I continued to say it after my father passed.

TJ came into the studio and it was his turn to get in the booth and lay it down for the completion of the (A) side of the project. I was very excited that it was finally done and we had more than enough music to shop. He was almost finished when my phone rung, this is a collect call from... then I heard my husband. I pressed 1 and I heard my husband say "Hey Mrs. B." I said "Hey there Mr. B." He said "Where are you?" I said "In the studio." He said "Everyone there?" I said "Yes." I put him on speaker and everyone said "What Up Antoine?" He said hello to everyone but he needed to talk to TJ, his artist. TJ went in the hallway while we continued to mix the (A) side of the album. It was about twenty minutes when TJ came back and told me Antoine will call me tonight.

Everything was complete and I sprung the good news on the team about the big event that was coming up. They were excited; so excited that some tears came down from Jannette's eyes and then we left the studio and went to eat.

It was 5:30pm and the day was done. I dropped everyone off at the train station and I went home to get prepared for my night at work. I got home by 7:00pm and I went into my mother's house, said hello and I ran upstairs to my house to get about 3 hours of sleep before going to work.

It was now 11:00pm; I got up, took a shower, put my uniform on and headed across the street to work. I took my ticket from the garage supervisor and went on to do my relays. I completed the 6 relays and went home to sleep until 8:00am. I got up, went to my job, signed out and went back home to sleep. The next few days I slept and worked on my regular schedule until Saturday morning when I got off of work and I went into the office to straighten out some contracts that Tanya had left for me to sign.

The next few weeks went by fast; between networking and open mics, talking to Antoine, and studio time. I did not even realize that we had completed the month of September and we were in the second week of October. That big event that I had invested in was soon arriving at the Apollo in two weeks for the Halloween weekend and after that weekend would be my second trailer visit with my husband.

The next two weeks I worked on getting the team together and that meant that they had to be perfect for the show because the entertainment companies; which where Wideworld Entertainment, Universal entertainment, and Barbour Entertainment, were having their artist performing as well for a recording contract. We had to press demos, souvenirs, and wrist bands, for giveaways so that the artists could have their names out in the world; as well as ring some alarms in the industry.

Saturday November 2, 1996
Apollo Theater "Music Industry Open Mics Blow Out"
12:00pm to 8:00pm
Fee: $20.00 tickets in advance, $30:00 at the door

We came in unity into the Apollo. I was surprised at how all the seats where filled and there was only standing room available. With the Apollo seating 1506 people I must say that the Uptown Promotion & Marketing team was very well the best team out there if you wanted a place filled. I walked over to Mr. Gerral and Hassan and shook their hands for such a great turn out.

People were in place, the artists, A&R, Record Label executives, the host Ed and the judges Chuck, Kevin, and Angelia. Ed, the host, started calling artists from the roster. Artists started performing and judges where judging the acts. Then it was TJ's turn, then DJ, and then they called Jannette, and then Samuel. I went to the judges to see how things were going. As I was leaving that area two of the A&Rs came to me and asked me about TJ so we spoke about TJ and set up a meeting at their offices. They were A&R from Def Jam and Sony. I continue to look at the acts and I notice this "Duo" (two young men) they were different; their names were "Ruff, Rugged and Real" from the Bronx. When they finished I walked over to them and I introduced myself to the two of them. The tall one, his name was Mike, he said "Mrs.B. you are the reason that we came to the open Mic." I was stunned! I said "What do you mean?" Mike said "We heard about how you are out here making things happen." I said "Thank you but how did you hear about me?" Then that's when the short one by the name of Kenny said "the streets are talking; especially when you don't play house."

I smiled and took it as a compliment, then I said "Good thing no one could even say they slept with me!" The boys then decide to meet with me in the office the following week for management. The night was coming to an end and the show was great. A lot of networking came out of this event and a lot of money was made that night; the numbers were sweet!! I had made my goal number $20,000 was my profit. HAHA straight to the bank!!!

It was now a week before my second trailer visit and I was getting things in order to take up; a list of things that Antoine wanted to eat and movies that we could watch. As the phone rang it was the Correction Dept. and so I pressed #1. Antoine was upset, I heard it in his voice so I ask "What is going on?" he said "I was expecting my trailer visit next week but I just got notice that they are moving me tomorrow." My heart dropped. I said "Where are you going?" Of course he could not tell me until he got there. I said "Did you get into a fight?" he said "No." I asked "Why are they moving you?" He said "Standard process when your charge categories drop in prison. He had been there for three years and his time was shorter now than longer so he had to go to another prison; a little closer to home. It was still a max prison but he had about 8 years left, so he had to be moved. I said "Ok Papi, don't get upset, wherever you go I will get trailer visits. He said '"It's not like that, you have to apply again." I said "So we'll do that." Antoine said "Mommy, I have to go work out so I can work off my anger." I said "I love you. Talk to you later." He said "Love you Mommy." I was very upset after the phone call but what could I do, it was not in my hands. This is something I could not fix.

I decide to take the meeting that was for TJ because before the phone call I was going to set the meeting up after my trailer visit. But now, it was on stand still so I called Def Jam Records and I asked to speak to Keith, the A&R for Rap artists. I did not want to sign TJ to Sony because that was a label that rooted into R&B and I know to get the best promotion and marketing for a rapper, he had to be with Def Jam. So as I waited for Keith to get on the phone I was crying. I really needed my husband at this time in my life. I was really making progress and what is success without someone to share it with? I was crying harder now than ever because I was thinking back on the movie "Mahogany"; the success Diana Ross had and her man was not there. How she fell into the slump of a drug addiction because she never wanted to cheat on Billy Dee; it hit me hard. As the voice said "Hello Mrs. B"; I cleared my throat from the tears and said "Hello Keith." I would like to schedule the meeting for Thursday with my artist at 2:00pm if that is ok with you? Keith said "Yes, that is good on my schedule." I said "Ok, see you then."

I hung up and fell in tears. The next few days I went to work without hearing from my husband. It was now Thursday, November 7th, and I was getting prepared to meet with Keith for my artist TJ's recording contract. I had got there about a half an hour earlier so that I would have the presentation perfect to get what I want; in the terms that was good for TJ.

I had on my Adrienne Vittadini black turtle neck jumpsuit that was fitting to my body with the wide legs, it came down to my ankle and I wore my Moschino pony print boots with my pony print wide belt and my pony printed clutch. My hair was in a full bun and I had on my diamond earrings, my necklace with one diamond that sat on my chest, and I always wore my beautiful wedding rings. I was always stunning and professional. It was my time to go into the conference room to negotiate the contract but TJ was still not present so we went on with throwing things in and out of the contract for about 30 minutes and I could not believe that TJ was still not there yet. This is what he always wanted, I called his phone; no answer. It was strange so I asked Keith could we adjourn this meeting for about an hour to see what was going on with my artist. He did not have anything on his schedule so Keith agreed because he had taken his other meeting in the early part of the day. As I continue to reach out to TJ his wife called me back and told me that they had a fight last night and he hit her so she called the police and TJ was in Rikers Island. I was shocked; with my mouth fully open; my mind was all over the place. I was trying to get my thoughts together to explain this to Keith, the A&R of Def Jam Records. I walked back into the conference room where Keith was and I said "I will have to adjourn this until further notice. There has been an accident with TJ, Keith said "Ok." and I said "I will call you Keith. Thank you." I was so upset I was done with the rap artist forever.

Chapter XXIX

November 8, 1996 -December 1996

Attica Correctional Facility

How Time Flies!!

It was Friday and I received my first call from my husband today about 3:00pm telling me that he is in Attica Correctional which is about an hour way from Clinton Correctional; but an hour closer to NYC. Of course I needed to find out what bus, or if Rosie's Van Service goes there, as well as get driving directions so I could drive to see him anytime I needed to. Especially now with this crazy stunt that TJ pulled. I was not happy; but I did not tell Antoine that I took the meeting because I did not want him to ask questions. That would be a discussion in our first visit at his new home in Attica. Funny how I accept his new home in this life that I was living. I learned to embrace my choice of living in the marriage that was laid out for me. I could not understand why GOD would want this for me but I knew it would get better.

Attica (639 Exchange Street Road), my new home of visitation. "It" was going to see me this weekend; in "Jesus" name I prayed that I would get there. I did not go the first weekend but the following weekend would be my long weekend off from work. I prepared to go see my husband;

I called Prison Gap bus company and made my reservation for Friday, November 15, 1996.

I continue to work that week and engage in a few open mics that I had Samuel and Jannette booked for small fees. I also worked with DJ on his new project. DJ was a rapper but much more humble and relaxed then TJ was. DJ had a friend, his name was Earl, that was impressed with "BBE" and how I ran the business. Earl was an engineer at "Chung King Studio"; one of the major recording studios in the music industry. Earl would let all my artists in the studio to lay their tracks and let them record there for a small fee. He would bill it to the company so their tracks were all mastered and mixed and ready to shop. It was a long week and now Friday was upon me. I pack my bags of course with the goods and a beautiful outfit so that I would always look good for my man. I pack everything in my candy apple red 4runner truck and was on my way to Columbus Circle to get on the bus to see the man of my life. I parked the truck in an overnight parking lot at 57th Street and walked to the bus. As I waited for the bus to arrive I saw some of the girls I use to ride with and we were kicking the breeze and then the bus arrived. I got on along with the girls that I knew, then a few others got on I continued to my seat. As I got on there was this young woman that got on too and she was talking to some of the women that I knew. Her name was Marsha, apparently she was in the music business but I had not known her so she was talking about the show that she was going to do and she was going to be MJB background singer. I just listened and did not say a word. I went on to sleep until the bus driver said the first stop will be Attica so get your stuff and be prepared to get off in about 30 minutes. I got my stuff and everyone else started to prepare as other started to wake up. I just sat until the bus stopped at Attica.

I took a look at my new surroundings and grabbed my stuff to exit the bus. As I exit the bus I notice that Marsha was exiting as well. I said "So your family member is incarcerated here?" Marsha said "No, my boyfriend." I say "Ok, I hope you have a good visit." Marsha said "Thanks, but who are you visiting?" I said "My husband." Marsha said "Is he new here?" I said "Yes, this is my first visit to this prison. My husband was in Clinton Marsha said "Ok, enjoy your visit." I said "Thanks."

I got in the building and it was nothing different; registration and then wait, but it seemed like my anxiety was high because I had so much to tell Antoine. My pressure was cooking; I was very excited to see him. I started to get hot and then I started to throw up.

Marsha came over and said "Mrs. B are you ok?" I said "No," She said "Did you eat?" I said "No." Marsha got some water for me and I drunk it and I felt better. I thanked her then my name was called.

I walk over to the C.O. to produce the marriage documents and all the other information that they needed. I walked into the waiting area to wait for Antoine. As Antoine walked over to me I was looking at "Billy Dee Williams" that's what he was to me. I was so happy to see my husband that I started to cry.

Antoine said "What's wrong Mommy?" I said "I missed you so much, I don't know if I could do this anymore!" I felt like "Mary J Blige" (I'm going down). Antoine said "What's on your mind?" I said "Let's just go to the machine; get all that you need because it going to be a long one. Antoine's look said, whatever you say Mrs. B, you are the boss!

As we sat down I raved about TJ and the deal I had on the table at Def Jam Records and that his butt was in Rikers Island and never showed up to sign the record contract that I fought so hard for; that was good for him, a person that just came from prison, hungry for success! How could he allow himself to be a victim. I said it all in one breath. Antoine said "Breathe Mommy, breathe." I went on to say that I am out here all alone with these freaking men in this industry that just want to freaking sleep with women that are weak and I am fighting them off every day.

Antoine's eyes light up and he said "What has happened that you have not told me?" Tears came down my eyes harder than ever and I said "Papi, you don't know how many times I was offered to go to men's house at night and they would guarantee me recording deals for my artist. But GOD has kept me faithful. That is what I have been telling you about GOD! He keeps me strong and all you think is it's just me. Why do you think I got SAVED! Years ago? I asked GOD for strength through your prison time and my business, you need to know that there is a GOD.

Antoine once again looked at me and said "YOU are my GOD, all I see is YOU!" I cried; in tears again and said "I am not your GOD, he lives inside of me, he keeps me coming here; those are the words I was raised on!"I DO!" I saw my mother and father together until GOD came to get his SON, my father and now I just have my mother to help with this walk."

Antoine went into deep thought and he asked "Do you want to take a break?" I said "No, I am going to continue the business." The investment on the Apollo show was good, my profit was $20,000.00. I'm going to do it next year again, but I am looking to do my 70's Players Ball next year as well. I partnered up with this promoting company,

"Uptown Marketing" that guarantees to sell out events. I added a new rap group to "BBE"; their names are Ruff, Rugged and Real. Antoine said "Anything else you would like me to know before this visit is over?" I said "Yes, I think I'm moving out of Staten Island to New Jersey, more for our money." Antoine said "What are you talking about?" I said "After Daddy died I sold my house and moved into a co-op building. I want my own house again, Baby, I know you are not home but I want to have everything laid out when you come home, so you never have to be in the street again. I will show you pictures of the house that I am looking at. It was now time to leave, the C.O. had come to our table, Antoine said, "How soon is this move?" I said "I will be looking at houses starting next week but we will be moving next year some time after the holidays." It was now time, I kissed him and left the visit.

I left the visit and I got on the bus. As I was going to the back one of the girls Renee asked me if Marsha talked to me. I said "Yes, we discussed her boyfriend."

Renee said "No she wants to talk to you about the business. I said we did not talk about that. Renee said "Mrs. B she knows everything that you do because she has been riding with us for about three months and we had told her about you, but you never got back on the bus and when you came Friday I told her that you where the woman we told her about." I said "Ok Thanks."

Marsha got on the bus from her visit and she asked Sara would she switch seats with her so that she could sit next to me. So Sara said yes. I was sitting down and Marsha said "Mrs., can I talk to you?" I said "Yes."

"Marsha Manning is my name" I said "Rafaela Barbour is mine." She said "Now that we are formally introduced, I would like to talk to you about what I'm doing and what

I need." Marsha was sharp; I had never run into an artist that was sharp at her craft. I was usually the educator. Marsha started talking about the year in the business and the people she opened up shows for, people that she had worked with, tours and travels. She was doing her thing so I could not imagine what she wants out of me. Marsha then said to me "So I heard from a lot of people, especially people that don't really know the business that you have an entertainment company and that you are a manager." I said "Yes, that I am." Marsha said "I don't have management and that is what I'm looking for." I said "You have been doing these things on your own?" Marsha said "Yes but I need someone that I could trust in the business to negotiate contracts because I see the difference with artist that have management; when it comes to money." Marsha said "I will be leaving for a week, going on tour with Mary J Blige, and when I come back I will be hosting at a club called Grooves in the Village. If I leave your name at the door as my guest will you come? I said "Yes." We talked some more and I handed her a business card and she gave me her phone number. The conversation was so refreshing after crying on the visit. We had arrived on 59th Street. I grab my bags and walk to 57th to get my truck and I drove home. I got in front of the door and my phone rang, it was Attica Correctional, I pressed the pound key and I heard Antoine say "So you think you're the man, making all these moves without talking to me first?" I said "Antoine you are not here, you won't be for a long time, so stop with feeling like you are not a part of this." Antoine said "Why would you buy a house without me and not let me get to decide what I like? I said "Because when you get here I don't know how things are going to be. Right now I have to make wise decisions and invest this money for the future. A house is a wise decision." We went back and forth with different things that occurred on this visit then I told him that he needs to miss me so I will not be coming up to see him until next year. I also spoke to him about what happened on the bus and he was very shocked that people on a prison bus was referring artists to me. Then a dial tone came on. I was not sure if he hung up or that's how the new phone system worked in Attica. Sunday I went shopping with my mother, as we always do and I got prepared for work. The rest of the week I went to work, talked to my husband and finally got him to see it my way. I spoke to Marsha a few times while she was away on tour, with various questions that she had, and then we spoke about her getting back to see her performance in the club. My week was complete and I was now content about my husband understanding the moves that were going to take place.

Chapter XXX

Club Grooves Open Mic

Marsha Manning Signs with Barbour Entertainment

Saturday, November 30, 1996, it was the weekend after Thanksgiving and the last Saturday of the month. It was the night that Marsha was going to host at Club Grooves. She had just come off a tour with MJB. I was at home getting ready to go the club and the phone rang, it was Marsha, she was calling just to see if I was still coming. I told her I will be there.

It was a cold night so I put on my burgundy Donna Karan knitted sweater dress that fell down to my ankles and my Diba Paisley Tapestry fabric knee high boots, the paisley had the colors of burgundy, brown, beige, and black. I throw on some of my nice jewelry and my hair was in a bun. I put my diamond earrings on; spray some Paloma Picasso fragrance, put on my mahogany mink jacket on and my brown Gucci bag. I got into the truck and was on my way to the club in the Village. It was a blessing when I got to the Grooves; there was parking on McDougal Street so I parked and walked to the door. It was a club right on the corner of Groove and McDougal. I walk in and it was pretty dark; the bar was to the right of me and the live entertainment was to the rear of the club. Marsha was on stage as I enter and she was performing one of Patti Labelle's songs "This Will Be an Everlasting Love" then Marsha spotted me coming through to get a seat closer to the stage. She smiled and then she continued to sing.

Marsha had a beautiful stage presence, she sang with grace and such personality that you could not do anything else but smile, she was like a grace of joy! I ordered my drink, some chicken and french fries. I continue to watch every artist that was there performing. I had not known that this was a place that artists, executives and A&R come to hang out after touring. This was their place of "Self being" where they could just sing and collaborate with each other. The air was fresh & free.

Marsha finished her song and she said I would like everyone to give a round of applause to my manager, Rafaela from Barbour Entertainment; for the very first time in my life I was speechless. I was so shocked my eyes rolled to the back of my neck. I was not prepared for this. I stood up and I thanked everyone for the introduction and I could do nothing other than smile with tears rolling down my eyes. Marsha got off the stage and introduced me to her mother. Marsha introduces me to some executives in the industry and we continued to enjoy the evening. It was about 2:30am, it was the end of the evening for me I had to get home to rest because Sunday was always my investor day to spend time with, "Hilda McEachin". My mother was my investor in Barbour Entertainment. She was my backbone, she had invested 40% of her earnings into my company and faithfully she had her money in. I won't ever disappoint her. I called Marsha as I was getting my coat and told her to call me at the office Monday. Marsha's response was "I will be at the office on Monday." I said "Ok, what time?" she said "About 3:00pm." I said "Well you would have to meet me at work." She said "Ok and I went over to Marsha's mother Sandy and said good night, it was a pleasure meeting you." She said "Rafaela, we will be seeing a lot of each other. I'm putting my daughter in your hands." I said "Thank you" and I left to return home to Staten Island.

Sunday morning bright and early Hilda was up at my house, "How was your night?" I started to tell Mommy what happen when the phone rang, it was Antoine, so I started to tell him what happened last night and he was just as shock as I was and Mommy said "Wow we have another artist on the roster? Fita, you are doing good." and I said 'Yes Mommy, we are doing good." I spoke to Antoine for about twenty minutes and the phone hung up. It was that Attica phone system; he called back and we spoke a little longer and I said "Papi I have to go. Mommy is waiting to leave." He said "Ok have a good shopping day." I said 'Ok thanks." Antoine never minds about my quality time with Mommy because he never lacked, whatever shopping I did, he received something too.

Hilda and I went shopping for things in the house and of course whatever else we wanted, then we ate out and came home early because we both had to get prepared for work it the morning.

Monday morning I went to work for eight o'clock and I did my route, came into the garage after I dumped the truck, went home, took a shower and prepared the Management contract so that when Marsha came to my job we would just wait for sign-out, go to the office and sign. Three o'clock on the dot Marsha was at my job. I introduced her to some of my coworkers and we left. Marsha and I went to the office. We discussed the contract and we signed on the dotted line. We went out to eat as a celebration; Marsha was ready to leave because she had a gig. The last gig that she would do without management's consent on the contract. I drove her to the ferry and I went home. There were now six artists on the roster. It was time for me to get a lawyer. I researched some lawyers and their backgrounds and I was very impressed with this woman name Stephanie. I called and left information for a return call.

The next few days went by as fast as I could blink and on Friday the Lawyer called me back as well as the Realtor, her name was Ashley that I was working with for housing.

December was a month of events and celebrations, I set up a consultation with the lawyer Stephanie on Monday and Ashley for Tuesday so it was going to be a busy month. The weekend came and I was going to an event Monique was hosting and she had the Wu Tang Clan performing on Bay Street at a club. It was a rap show so I decide I would dress down. I wore my biege and brown Gucci mini dress that fell to the knees and my knee high Gucci boots with the brown G's, put on gold jewerly and put my hair in a ponytail. I did not wear a coat, it was close to home, I just parked and ran into the club. It was crowded and there was so many people behind stage. I could not believe all of them were part of the Clan. I walked to the bar to get a drink and I heard this Jamaican guy chanting, I listened close and oh my he was good. I hand him a card and ask him to call me.He said "Ok my name is "Linkx". I said "Rafeala" He said "I will call you tomorrow." I agreed and I went backstage with Monique and continued to network. I enjoyed the show and about 2:30am I told Monique that I was leaving. I was very tired.

Chapter XXXI

Linkx Signing with BBE

Maplewood Purchase

Sunday morning came and I had not received Linkx's call and that was ok by me because I know that I had to work Sunday evening; back on the midnight tour. I could not wait to get seniority on Staten Island because my life was like a merry go round, not having a set schedule was so much, but I handled it. I did my relays and went home to sleep; it was about 8:30am the phone rang and it was my supervisor "Are you coming to sign out?" he asked. I said "Yes" and he said "Don't forget the tickets." I said "Ok."

I put my pajamas on and ran across the street to hand my tickets in and sign out. I went home and got back in the bed until about 11:00am. I jumped in the shower and I pulled out my olive green vintage two piece skirt suit, french coffee stockings and my black Nina Ricci pumps. I put my hair in a ponytail, put my gold knot earrings on, grabbed my black Gucci bag and put my black mink coat on. I jumped in my truck to Manhattan to see the lawyer. I had a 3:00pm appointment. I got to the city about 2:15pm. I went to a parking lot that was across the street from the lawyer's office on 56th Street and Park Avenue.

Stephanie's office was located at 432 Park Avenue on the 10th floor. I walk into the building, got on the elevator and when I got to the 10th floor it was a very elegant layout. The receptionist was very pleasant. I said 'Hello I'm Rafaela Barbour and I have a 3:00pm with Stephanie." She said "Ok please have a seat, I will let her know you are here, I said "Thanks."

Stephanie came out and said "Hello Rafaela, how are you?" I responded and said I am doing fine and yourself? She said "I'm well, so let's go to my office." I followed Stephanie to her office. I couldn't believe that her office was laid out like a conference room. "I was in the big league now" I sat at the top of the table and she sat on the other end of the table like the Sopranos. I looked at the decor on her walls and for sure I knew she was expensive but the money was well earned; she was sharp at her craft. Stephanie asked me a few question on the business and my financial status of the business. She explained the service that she would render and what her fees were. She talked about what she would also provide if necessary and I agreed. We agreed on the terms and how long she would provide the service. Our meeting was good and I got to know who she was and vice a versa. We exchanged cards as we adjourned the meeting at 5:30pm. I left the building, picked up my truck and headed home. I needed to get some sleep before going to work for the midnight shift.

Tuesday morning I left my job and went to sleep because I knew that Ashley, the realtor was going to call me about 12:00pm. I got up about 11:00am and got in the shower. I wanted to be ready just in case she had something for me to look at, but in the mean time I had called my mother Hilda. She was always saying that I was not doing anything constructive like having dinner ready for her when she came home. Being that I was on the midnight shift and home all day, I called her and I told her that I was going to cook so that she would not have to have an attitude when she got home with me. 12:00pm came and went and no Ashley. So I decide to go to Pathmark on Foster Avenue to pick up something to cook. As I got in the truck my cell phone rung, it was Ashley. She said "Hello Rafaela, sorry for the delay but I have found a couple of houses for you to look at." I said that was fine and I asked her when would we be looking at them. Ashley said "Now, I am getting off the Verrazano Bridge as we speak. I will be to your house in about five minutes. I agree and totally forgot where I was going.

Ashley arrived at my house and she said "I will be driving so put your car back in the garage." I put my truck back in the garage and I got in Ashley's car. We headed to New Jersey, the first two houses were in Newark, the third was in Jersey City. I then said "Ashley, I want a house with a lot of land and I don't want to be attached to my neighbors. I want a garage, and I don't want to move to a house that I have to move out in two years because the neighborhood is bad." She said "I understand." So I said "Is there anything else?"

Ashley made a phone call to the broker's office and he had given her two other houses. They were in Maplewood, New Jersey. Ashley drove to Maplewood and I said "This is what I am talking about. This is more me. We drive up to one of the houses, it was on Yale Street, off of Springfield and it was very nice. Two levels and a back yard, and it was a detached house, but it was not what I wanted so Ashley continued to drive more into the Maplewood area. She drove and we got in front of a house that in my heart I knew it was mine. You know when it is yours; when it feels like home.

Ashley said "Rafaela I have a confession to make. I said "What Ashley?" she said "You see that house? I said "YES!!! That is what I was talking about." Ashley said "Well we just got this house on our MLS listing but there is a problem." I looked at her and said what's the problem? Ashley said I don't have the key to show it to you. I said "Are you kidding me? She said "No when I called in they gave me the address to this house but I have no key. Ashley looked at me and saw that I was in love with this house just from the outside and said look if you don't tell I won't tell." We got out of the car and walk to the backyard. There was a door and the top of it was glass near the locks. Ashley busts the glass and we were in the property. This house was immaculate. It was a two family house, full finish basement, four car garage and up above the garage was a studio apartment. The house was two levels in the first apartment, and on the other side there was a door for the second floor apartment; a three bedroom on the top, it was detached, and it had a back yard that sat on a half of acre of land. I was sold.

I had broken into my future house with the agent. I started to cry. Ashley said "What is wrong?" It was tears of joy." I said. "I want it!" Ashley said "Ok." She called into the broker and said that I want to purchase the house. I could read the conversation, the broker must have asked Ashley "How did you get to see the inside? Ashley's response: the back door was broken. We both laughed and went to the car to fill out the papers. It was now about 6:30pm and my phone rang, it was my mother mad as heck about her dinner. I said Mommy; I am sorry I will explain it when I get home, Hilda was mad and hung up.

Ashley continued to fill out the papers in the car and told me that I had to come in with my mother Friday just to get all other major information that we need to submit on the application before going into closing I agreed, and then Ashley started driving to get me home. I did not think that it was going to be all that bad after I tell my mother that I did not cook but I bought her a house.

I got back home and I thank Ashley for my house. I went into the building and said hello to the door man out by the elevator and pressed 4, I walked into the house. Hilda had an attitude and I said "Mommy I am sorry. I did not know that the realtor was going to come late but I have a surprise for you." Hilda said "What? You have dinner?" I said no Mommy better than that, Hilda said "What Rafaela?" I knew she was really mad. She only calls me Rafaela when she is boiling inside. Well Mommy, I did not get dinner but I bought you a house." "Rafaela, you are the only person I know that goes out food shopping and buys a house." Hilda said. But then she smiled and said "Where on Staten Island, are we moving to?' I said "It is in New Jersey." Hilda really was mad then, yelling "How am I going to get to work in the morning?" I said "We will work it out, I promise you Mommy. You are going to love this house, I will drive you to see it tomorrow." We continued to talk and ordered Chinese food and enjoyed the evening.

On Wednesday I called Ashley to see if she was available to show my mother the house. Ashley said I could come about 6:00pm and I will have the key. My mother left her job early and was home at 5:30pm. At 6:00pm Ashley arrived and we went to Maplewood, New Jersey but this time we went in my truck so that I could drive to my new house; and I needed to learn how to get there. We arrive at 127 Union Avenue in Maplewood, NJ; to my new residence and Ashley opened the door. That was all she wrote, Hilda was in love with the house. After leaving we went through the neighborhood to get the feel of the neighborhood and then we left and came back to Staten Island and Ashley reminded me, "Rafaela you and your mother have to come into the office on Friday to sign papers and copy the documents." We both agreed. We went upstairs and my mother was happy and said "Thanks Fita. I love the house. When are we moving?" I said "If we could close by Christmas we could move in the first of January."

Ashley called me on Wednesday night and asked me if I had any people to refer to her. I said "Yes Ashley, I don't want to be alone in N.J., so my cousin and her husband are looking to buy a house." I gave Ashley Clarissa and Sean's information. Clarissa and Sean went to see the house on Yale Avenue and bought it so I was not alone. My family was a few block away.

The week before Christmas we closed on the house and we both said "Merry Christmas" (Mommy and I). That weekend I went to see my husband and I told him everything that had occurred the last few weeks. Antoine was happy but I know that it bother him that he could not participate in anything; that's what was happening in my life because he was locked up and it was not the same as being free with your wife making moves for the better of your life.

Chapter XXXII

Attica Correctional

January 1997

It was now the "New Year" and I had purchased a beautiful home for my mother and some day for my husband to spend the rest of our lives. I was still living in Staten Island and I had paid my first mortgage payment and still had to pay rental fees in my apartment in Staten Island. My business was booming and I did not have time to pack. My mother had her stuff packed but I was in the midst of contracting my artists to go on tour. I was working, going to the studio with "Linkx" and "Yankee Bee," "Ruff Roughed and Real" was going on the road so I was tied up and could not pack. "Janetta" was singing background and "Samuel" was singing in little bars all over town. "DJ" was on tour with the group MOP and "TJ" was in prison missing it all. "Marsha" was getting ready to go back on tour with MJB and she wanted me to go so I had called my cousin Clarissa to see if her and her husband Sean could help me move. Her response was "We moved to our house Christmas Day." I said "Congrats!" I told my mother that and she was upset because that meant that her sister Sarah, my aunt, was already in New Jersey because my cousin had took her mother as well. After the conversation with my cousin I realized that it was time to move. I called a moving company and schedule a moving date for the last weekend in January which was two weeks from today so that I would have everything in order. You know all my I's would be dotted and all my T's would be crossed. I did not want to forget or miss any money.

It was at this point, the second weekend of January that I went to see my husband. I was overwhelmed and needed a boost of love. So I took out my LV duffle bag and I put in my Yves Saint Lauren black crush velvet suit with a tiger print top, my black riding boots, with my Victoria under garments and white diamond perfume, some jewelry and my small Gucci change bag. My hair was in box braids so I could design any style that I wanted when I got there. I got in the truck and being that I had not made any reservation by bus, it was going to be my first driving adventure to Attica. I got on the 440N / W Shore Expressway to I-80 West to I-380 North to I-81 to 17 West to Groveland Exit 6 to I-390 to NY36 North and there I was at Attica. It was about eight and a half hours but I was happy to have gotten there. I thought I would never get there so I drove into the prison parking lot and walked to the building.

I got on line and I registered. As I waited the Correction Officer had called me so when I got up he asked me for some information that was not on my file. I asked him what was that information for and he responded "For your family visit application." I said "Ok." He then said "Your husband had put it in so there was some information we had to get from you." I say "Ok thank you." I walked into the visiting floor to wait on my husband who would be coming down shortly. Antoine always looked so good when he came down. Not only was I sharp but he was so handsome, my Papi for life, and I just wanted to eat him up every time I saw him. But of course, I was very controlling. If anything, I was learning my biggest lesson. I wasn't in control because I was married at this point to a man that was facing seven more years. The eight years that had gone by us was a struggle but I got through it. Antoine came and I got up to kiss him because it had been a few weeks since my last visit. I needed to stand and hug to get some of the good feel of my "Big Daddy"; that's was what I called his penis. I had not had any since the trailer visit. After I got a feel of Big Daddy we went straight to the vending machine to get our regular meal; six packs of wings, four bags of french fries, three cans of Pepsi, three chocolate bars, and two bags of popcorn. We took our meal to the appointed seat and we went straight into business. Antoine's first question was always; "How is Mommy?" I said fine. "How is my mother?" I said "She fine, I spoke to her yesterday." "How is the house?" I laughed and said "I don't know." Antoine looked and said What do you mean?" I said "I have not moved in yet." Antoine said "what are you waiting for?" I said "There is so much on my plate. I don't have time to move." "Where is the house?" "New Jersey." So Mrs. Barbour you moved us out to New Jersey? "Yes, it's a beauty. I then said "look" and I showed him the pictures and he was very impressed. Antoine said "Mommy that's a lot of land and a very big house. I said "it is even bigger inside." Antoine said "so you want to move to N.J. because?" I said everyone that I am involved within the industry has invested in N.J. and you get more for your money."

Antoine said "I guess Monique is in N.J. being that you and her are close. The Clan has their mansion out there and you also got family out there. That's good. I said "Yes." We spoke on the mortgage amount and all the expenses and when I schedule the move we agreed to all of that. Antoine then hit me with a new connect he had uptown that I had to meet so that money will be coming in. I agree to meet the following weekend after the move. It was going to be a real sensitive situation because I had to go alone and it would be late. I knew that I would be okay because Antoine would never put me in a dangerous situation and people knew Antoine and how he roll so they did not mess with him about his money. We spoke on a few more things about BBE and the artist and plans for a big event that I was putting together but it would be down the road; called the 70"s Players Ball. By this time the visit was over. I got up, kissed Antoine and left. I never ever looked back once I got up. It was just something I could not do.

Chapter XXXIII

To My White House

Moving to 127 Union Ave, Maplewood New Jersey

The following week was very hectic. I went to work, went to the studio, meetings, completed the move to my new house, then I left to meet the people uptown, and I got everything in place for the money to start rolling in. I was on my way home to Staten Island and realized that I had moved and I had to turn around and go through the George Washington bridge to my house. It was just a crazy weekend and by the time I got home I just went to sleep on the floor; it was fully carpeted with very thick rugs.

Monday morning I got up, got in the shower, got dressed, and went outside on the other side of the house to my mother's apartment upstairs. We both had taken off from work for a week to get things in place at the house. I went to her house and asked did the moving men ever come. She said "No, I called and did not get an answer, so I was not feeling good about this. I called the number on the receipt and it was disconnected. I was mad by now because I knew that I was robbed. I called the Better Business Bureau and talked to a representative and explained everything that took place during the move. When I gave her the name of the company she said "Mrs. Barbour that company has been out of business for two years." I was hurt, but mad that they were still in the Yellow Pages because that is where I got the information from. I looked at my mother and said "Mommy, we have been robbed. That company stole all the furniture. My mother started speaking in Spanish; cursing actually and then she laughed. That was her way of showing her anger, we both started to laugh and then we started to cry. She said to me "Fita, what are we going to do? I said "Mommy lets just go shopping." I was a woman that never told my left hand what my right hand was doing. I was an investor of many companies, I was my father's daughter and he was a man with many incomes. My mother was a saver as well; so we got in the truck and made the best of the week that we had off.

The first day was good, my mother and I went to buy bedroom sets. Hilda wanted to go to Staten Island to this warehouse that sold colonial wood bedroom sets, then we went to National Liquidators where she bought her cooking utensils, and then it was my time up to buy what I wanted. I had found a store in N.J. on Route 22 called Bed Unlimited where they sold unique stuff and I was always someone that liked my things to be different from the rest. I bought a king size cream leather bedroom set with glass. It had a stereo on the backboard. It was gorgeous. The deliveries were scheduled for the next day so we had to sleep one more day without beds. By this time it was about 7:00pm so on our way home we decide to go to my cousin Tata's (Clarissa's nick name) house on Yale to see how they were coming along with their house. My mother had never seen their house so it was going to be her first time. I saw the house before it was bought. As we got to the house my mother was impressed, she said "This town has a lot of beautiful homes. I agreed, pulled up in the driveway, rung the bell, and my aunt Sarah answered the door. She was so happy to see my mother nevertheless a familiar face in front of the door. Walking in, my cousin Tata came down an asked "Did you move in to your house?" I said "Yes." Then we got to talking about what happened to us during the move. We all laughed and had a lot of jokes about the move, they were happy for us and we left.

Tuesday the delivery arrived and Mommy was upstairs with her stuff and I was downstairs doing my stuff. Wednesday came we went to get some paint and some more stuff for the house.

Thursday Antoine called and I told him what happened. He was upset but he laughed, then he told me to take money out of the bank; the account that was set up for emergencies. He said "Go get the living room set." Mommy and I went shopping for the living room sets and some stuff for the bathrooms. That was most of our Thursday and Friday. Saturday we just worked on the house and waited for deliveries. It was an experience that I would never forget.

Sunday we rested all day. I talked to Antoine and my mother cooked. Tata, TiTi and Sean came over for movie night.

My mother and her sister Sarah decide to start planning how they would commute back and forth into the city to work; being that they did not drive.

Ten o'clock came and everyone left. I went downstairs to my house and to bed. I had to be to work for 6:00am Monday.

February was now upon us and the weather was getting very cold. Snow was approaching us; with me working and then dealing with the snow storms, I was working twelve hour shifts and still maintaining Barbour Entertainment, the artist's schedules, the tours, the royalty checks, and the road shows. I also was checking on the money from uptown; the other business that was my husband's investment. I was tired all the time but I knew that this is the life I dreamt of and building; I could not stop. I would do everything to live this life that was giving to me more opportunities.

March came, as well as April with everything going smoothly I did not realized that it was time for my second trailer visit; but my first in Attica Correctional. Antoine called me like he usually does but it was a different kind of approach. He said "Mommy where are you?" I said "Home." He said "When are you leaving?" I said "For what Antoine?" He said "You forgot our trailer visit is this week?" I said "Papi, it is Thursday, May 2nd - Saturday, May 5th. What are you all crazy about?" He said "Because it's Tuesday." I said "Oh. There has been so much that I have been doing the last two months with this house and the damn snow. I have been blowing for the City of New York then coming home and blowing out this snow on the house. You have no idea how much work this is." Antoine said "With all that land you did not invest in a snow blower? Well Mrs. B, it does not take a rocket scientist to figure out that you should have bought one by now." I said "Ok Baby, let me get in the shower and call me back in an hour. I will be dressed and ready to get the stuff that we need for the trailer visit so that I could pack and leave. In an hour I was dressed. The phone rang and Antoine gave me his list of what he wanted to eat and I was off the phone.

I picked up the meats first, then the vegetables, the drinks, the cake and the sweets at Pathmark on Valley Avenue. Then I swung over to Livingston Mall and went into the adult toy store. Last, I went to Victoria Secret to get a few sets. Then I went home and I packed everything that I wanted to take with me. I had to do all that I could because I was going to work for midnight tonight and when I got off work I could only get about six hours of sleep before driving up for my trailer visit. I did not worry about my hair because I had just got it done in braids a week ago and my nails and toes also; so I was set. I got back in the house and I ate my dinner. I laid down until 10:30pm, left my house and went to visit my mother for a second, and then I went to work. I went to work as I usually do; I did my six relays and turned the tickets in. This time I just signed out. I did not worry about the few hours that I was losing. It would save me some time. I left the job and went home to sleep. It was about 3:00pm when I woke up so it was still a little early for me to start driving. I called my mother and I spoke to Hilda. I told her that I would be leaving for my trailer visit and wouldn't be returning until Saturday. She said "Ok." I also surprised her and said "Well if you come straight home there will be some dinner prepared at my house, so use your key and eat. Love you Mommy. I will see you when I come back."

Chapter XXXIV

Attica Correctional Family Visit

It was Thursday about 7:00am; I had reached my destination to Attica. Surprisingly I was not tired. The drive was smooth; no real traffic. It was a day that I always looked forward to, spending two nights and three days with my husband. What a way to enjoy married life but I accepted it; for I was in love with this man. As I waited to be called there were a few young women in front of me and two other full families with their children.

I wait as they called the first young woman and told her she could not get on her trailer visit. She was devastated. I started to get scared, my heart was pumping; is this how Attica do their trailers? Not letting families know beforehand. That was not a nice way to find out that your family visit was not approved. I just sat in my chair praying that would not be my situation because my husband was a crazy motherf__ and I don't know what happens back there. The C.O.s (Correction Officers) continue to call the other women and the families as well and they got on the bus to be taken to their trailers.

An hour later the C.O. returned and I was the next one to be called but they called the family behind me. I was really worried by then, they called two other families. I was devastated by now and tears started to roll down my face.

The C.O. came over to me and asked me "Mrs. Barbour what's wrong?" I looked at him and asked if my husband was alright and if I was still getting my trailer visit. The C.O. looked deep into my eyes and as I saw him catch his breath he said "Yes your husband is not ready, he is in the shower." I looked up to the sky and said thank you GOD my trip was not a waste, I then waited until they called me. It was about twenty minutes later that they had called my name and the C.O. said "Mrs. Barbour were you crying because you thought that your trailer was taken from you?" I responded "Yes" The C.O. then said "We do our trailer different than the ones you have been on, your husband is in the trailer before you are at Attica." I thank him for telling me the standard process and continue to walk on the bus.

Attica's trailer was a little different from Clinton's trailer. Attica's Trailers were two family trailers side by side. Then the next one was in front of you or behind you but they were all in the same area. I got into the trailer and before I could put the bags down Antoine was at the door buck naked all over me. We never made it to the bedroom nor pass the doorway. I guess my husband was in a very horny mood. Antoine pulled my clothes off and I had never been eaten like this in my life. It was like a snake in the grass, licking and licking. I then laid down on the rug at the door way and he went inside of me like I never felt before. It was like me in water trying to swim; we made love at the doorway for about two hours, experienced different positions and then we both screamed out loud. He said "Mommy" and I said "Papi" and it was done. We had fulfilled our desire for one another and it was over. My husband and I got up and got in the shower and went to bed to talk; but of course we both fell asleep.

We woke up to the door bell ringing like something had happened and Antoine went to the door. It was the C.O. (Correction Officer). He walked in and said is everything alright in here? And where is your wife? Antoine said "In the bedroom. The C.O. said "I need to see her." Antoine came in and said get dressed and goes out to the living room. As I got dressed the C.O. came in the bedroom as Antoine was leaving out.

Antoine said "Officer, what's the problem? My wife is ok." He said, we called twice, once every hour and no answer. Antoine said "We were asleep" and the C.O. said "It is still day time and this is stand procedures if you don't answer during visiting hours. We don't come after 11:00pm because those are sleeping hours. Antoine said "Ok. Understood." The officer said "Thank you, have a nice family visit." and he left.

I went to the kitchen, I cooked dinner, we ate and watched some TV. About 10:00 we went back to the bedroom and made love. At 4:00am we went to sleep. It was 8:00am when the phone rang; it was the CO checking in; Every hour on the hour, the whole day, so we just enjoyed the living room on that Friday. We did everything that could have been done in the living room from eating to love making to eating our desserts on the tables, chairs, floor, and counter top. Everything that weekend had my a__on it. I was his wife, the stripper, girlfriend, and mistress. I was everything that a man desired in his life time; that's what I was to my husband and role playing was very big for us.

It was Friday evening when the C.O. knocked on the door about 7:30pm and asked could they come in. Antoine said "Sure, just wait". Antoine came into the living and said "Mommy go put some clothes on." I went to put clothes on in the bedroom and walked back into the living room. The C.O. looked at me and Antoine. "How long did you guys stay up last night?" So we both said until about 4:00am. The C.O. asked "Did you guys hear anything strange?" We both said "No." The C.O. said that they were going to dismiss the trailer visits a day early, meaning that I would have to leave in the morning. I would not have one more night. So I ask the C.O. why? Did we do anything to violate the rules? The C.O. said "Mrs. Barbour it is neither you nor your husband. You guys enjoy yourself, but the family next door was found dead... I screamed and Antoine said "WHAT!" The C.O. said this is not a good sign. The State might stop family visits. I asked the C.O. "How?" I was shock. The C.O. said they did not answer the phone for two hours and when we went to check the wife was in the bathroom dead, the kids in their rooms, and the inmate was in the bedroom dead. The C.O. said you and your husband have to pack. We will move you to another empty trailer and everyone will leave in the morning. As we walk to the door to close the door we saw all the police cars, State Troopers, Medical examiner, and Warden. Everyone was right next door and my husband and I was so in the midst of enjoying ourselves we did not hear anything. Just in tuned with US! An hour later another C.O. came to pick us up and take us to another trailer. That night I could not sleep. Antoine and I stayed up talking about us, because we never wanted to end up like that. We talked about the business plans and the thing that where going to happen. I told him about the 70's Players Ball and what I wanted to take place, the radio station, the artists and the games. We laughed but still came back to the conversation about the family next door. I laid in my husband's arms and finally we fell asleep. But before I could get really into my sleep the C.O. knocked on the door and we were departing. I kissed him and got on the bus. It was Saturday and it was early. I would have usually stayed to get on the visit but they had cancelled all visits that Saturday. So the buses had to go back. I got in my truck and drove home. I got home about 8:00pm and I went straight to my mother's house. She was shocked to see me but I could not wait to share what had happened and Hilda was holding me so tight. She said "It could have been you if you and your husband did not have a great relationship." I looked at my mother and said "What are you talking about Mommy?" she said "Fita, that was a relationship that went bad." I had dinner, talked a bit, and then went upstairs to rest.

The next day Antoine call me and of course he had the information on what happened and he said just what Mommy had said but Antoine had the specifics. Antoine said the wife was having a relationship with some man on the outside and the husband found out and waited for her to come up on the trailer visit with the kids.

Antoine then said "I put us in for three or four more trailer visits this year but I do not know when we will get them." I said "Ok, just let me know beforehand so I get those dates off on my job." We talked some more and the phone hung up. I talked to Antoine again in the evening, then I got prepare to go to work for the next day.

The next few weeks came and went with me talking to my husband, going to the studio and continuing to build my brand in the industry. I continued to go to showcases and networking parties with my artists; they were performing in different places and of course my money was straight in all ways.

It was now starting to get warm and the time was changing where it would get dark later; about 8:30pm and

New York City started to get live again. But of course, it was time for me to get off with my husband. It was his birthday week when we had gotten our next trailer. His birthday was the 11th of June and mine was the 5th of June. I had gotten a trailer for June 12th, and I was going to be a real hot Momma. I got up to Attica and every C.O. was saying happy belated birthday. I guess Antoine was telling everyone that our birthdays were 6 days apart and we got the trailer a day after his birthday so I brought him a birthday cake. I was so glad the Attica was not like Clinton with the cake because I gave Antoine his cake without a hand print in it. I got into the trailer and the light was off and I said "Ok Antoine lets stop playing. Antoine came out with frosting all on Big Daddy. He had stuck it in the cake and so I did what most people do; I ate the cake and the frosting off of Big Daddy; that was all she wrote. We continued where we left off on the trailer visit before. It was an every hole weekend. I did not bring any clothes with me for this trailer. We had so much fun that the trailer visit had ended so fast. I was packing before I realized that three days had gone by.

It was the middle of June and I had been spending a lot of money on the things that needed to be done but it was now time to get on the grind because I was having my first annual 70's Players Ball and I had to have my numbers(money) right. So Antoine went on his grind and so did I. I worked my job and his business; wherever I needed to go to pick up money, I was there.

I booked the 6 artist that I had and I got my 20%. It was a win-win situation and everyone was happy. I booked other artists, and I negotiated contracts for other artists and then I took my finders fee. I was into everything that my brain was capable of. It was now August 1st and it was 47 days before the 70's Players Ball. Everyone needed to get half of their money. I had, Bugsy, DJ Red Alert from Hot 97, Ralph Mc Daniels from Video Music Box and everyone was on board. Part of the bill (party) had gotten paid so I was good.

I had Clan, Teflon, and a couple of others coming through. My girl Monique from the WU salon, and Lesha from the Brenda Salon. It was a big event and it was going down on September 13th, the second Saturday of the month.

I worked the rest of August and September came right on in. The first week of September, I visited my husband. It was great and the next week was the "Players Ball". That week my mother and his mother went to surprise him while I had the event.

The Players Ball was at "Club Demarara" it was on 28th Street between 7th and 8th in Manhattan. It was three floors. I had two DJs but the main floor was Red Alert, Bugsy as the Host and Ralph put it on Video Music Box. I had the games from the 70's that we played, and the talent performance, it ran smooth. It was a success and I had sold out to capacity, 1,500 people showed up and I made good money.

The Player's Ball had gone by and it seemed as though the year was almost over. I had gotten two more trailer visits at Attica. It was a blessing that I got a trailer visit on Halloween week and I had my trailer visit on Thanksgiving. Christmas went by and the New Year came sneaking in; Happy New Years! 1998

I got my New Years call early in the morning. It was my husband and I was so happy to hear from him. Then he said "Well I am glad that we got a few trailer visits in because I will be moving. I said "Don't stress, we will get trailer visits.

Antoine said "NO we won't!" I said "Why?" He said "Baby, I have five years left and I will be home. Ten years went by and it is count down time. I said "Five years is not count down time." He said "It is in the prison world. I will be moving by the end of the week to Groveland Correctional and there is no trailer visits. "That is a medium security prison." I said and Antoine said "And you don't get family visits at medium prison." I said "OK."

We continue to talk until the phone cut off.

Chapter XXXV

Groveland Correctional Facility

I had been sick for about a week I could not hold anything down. I kept throwing up and my body did not feel right, working at night and sleeping during my shift was not right to me so I decide to go to the doctor. I told the doctor that I had mood swings and I could not keep food down. The doctor said "Could you be pregnant? I said "No." He said "Are you on birth control?" I said "No." He said "When was your last sexual encounter?" I said "Thanksgiving week." He said "So why do you feel that you could not be pregnant Mrs. Barbour?"I said "Because it didn't cross my mind. I never got pregnant during any other trailer visits, why should I be pregnant now?" Doctor said "Ok Mrs. Barbour, if you're so sure, lets take a pregnancy test," Sure as you had sex... I was pregnant; I was 8 weeks.

It was about a week or two before my husband called me. When they moved him from one prison to the next it was standard procedure in the correctional system that you had no communication with the inmates. It was the second week of the New Year that I got his first call from Groveland Correctional. We talked and he told me how it was a different type of setting and the do's and don'ts, I told him that I would be there this weekend to see him. He was very happy for such a visit. We talked and a voice like a recorded message was heard on the phone; the call will be disconnected in two minutes. Antoine said "Mommy, I will call you on Thursday before you come up. I said "Ok, I love you." and he said the same.

I worked the rest of the week and talked to Antoine. By Friday I was on my way to see him. I had to drive because I was not sure what bus or train would go there. I got on I-78 W in Millburn from Parker Avenue. Take I-80 W, I-380 N, I-81 N, NY-17 W and I-390 N to NY-36 N in Groveland. Take exit 6 from I390 N. The entire trip took 4 hours and 26 minutes. Here I was at the facility that would be the last of Upstate New York prison time. "Groveland" Correctional Facility, this was a facility with no trailer visits and he would be here for the duration of his time before coming back downtown to the City. This was my new home for the next five years. He was coming home in 2003; it was 1998. I could not believe that I had just done 10 years of this prison sentence with my husband. It seemed like yesterday, that I heard the judge say 7 to 14 years. I remember that clearly and I was not sure if I could have survived this 15 years, But through the GLORY of GOD I had made it, and faithfully.

I was at the front of the facility and of course there where forms to fill out and you had to produce documents for verification. After that process it was a waiting game, so by the time I got to see my husband it was about 10:00am and mind you I was there at 7:00am visits; start at 8:00am. I got to the visiting table and Antoine was there. We went to get the food first as we usually do, which meant there was going to be a lot of talking. I was going to tell Antoine the good news of our pregnancy. So as we sat down I said "I have something to tell you." Antoine said "What is it?" "WE are Pregnant!!!" Antoine looked at me and said "Are you for real?" I laughed and said "Yes." I handed him the picture of the baby inside of me and he just smiled. Tears ran down his face and he said "I don't think you should be doing a lot. You know how you are a high risk so, some of those stressful duties will be lifted off you. I looked and said "I am good."

Well as you know the whole visit was about my pregnancy and what is best. Antoine was now a proud father-to-be and he was smiling the whole time.

The visit was over. I left as I normally do; where I kiss him and never look back. That was my way of being able to stay strong. It was time to get the very important things in order like who was going to be the person that would bring work to him. Who would I allow to get that close to him? I decide to talk to a young woman that I know. Her man was on Antoine side, so she could take work to him, so no one would be in my husband face. The young woman would be taking it to her man and Antoine would be getting it from him.

It was now about March and I was about 16 weeks into my pregnancy when I got the bad news about my brother-in-law Roger. He had gotten shot in Mississippi, and I had to be the one to give Antoine the news about his brother. I figured if Marjorie went with me it would be easy. Marjorie was Antoine's mother. I drove up to Groveland Correctional on that Saturday. It was a surprise visit. I did not tell him his mother was going to be on the visit so he was happy when he got on the visit. I settle in like usual and we started eating and that is when his mother looked at him and said I have something to tell you. Antoine said "What Mommy." Marjorie then looks at him and said "Roger got shot in his house in Mississippi." and Antoine said "Is he ok?" Marjorie looked at me and I said "Papi, he did not survive." Antoine screamed, "NO, NO, NO." It was the last thing Antoine said then the tears ran down his face. He had dismissed himself from the visit and we left. I know that he needed some time to get himself together. That was his baby brother. Antoine was the oldest and had left two brothers in the street with his mother and now he only had Trevon, the baby left. We left and I drove back home as I prayed that he would prepare to come to the funeral. Monday I would make the call to the facility. Antoine came down for the funeral and went back.

The next month, April 1998, I went to see Antoine and coming from the visit I had gotten into an accident on the Verrazano Bridge and a tractor trailer truck hit me from the rear; completely moving my vehicle away from the toll booth. I was hospitalized and I had lost the baby; leaving me in shock and in depression. Also leaving me with injuries to my breast, head, and bleeding from my vagina. It was a bad accident.

Chapter XXXVI

The Accident

The next month it was April 1998, I went to see Antoine at Groveland Correctional; coming back from the visit, I had gotten into a car accident on the Verrazano Bridge. I remember a Tractor Trailer truck hit me from the rear; completely moving my vehicle from the toll booth. I could remember hitting my head on the steering wheel, along with my breast and my stomach. I was taken to the hospital. I was hospitalized for a few days with the result of losing my unborn child. I was in shock when they told me about my baby. I went straight into a depression. I was very heart broken; it had been the fifth child that I lost from my husband. My depression was with question of the abortion that I had years ago when GOD had bless me with twins that was not Antoine but for the love that I had for Antoine I aborted those twins. My life had become bitter sweet, I flat-lined after that for a few months.

In the month of not going to see my husband and in my recovery, I had a friend of mine come to check up on me. He had heard that I was in an accident. His name was Mr. Biggs. Mr. Biggs was my girlfriend Yvonne's cousin Brandy's boyfriend, she was in love with this man; he was cool with me and he even helped me move some of my stuff from Staten Island to New Jersey; so he knew where I lived. Mr. Biggs said "Brandy asked me to check up on you to see if you needed anything; being that you have not been able to get around", I said "No thanks Mr. Biggs." He then repeated, "If you need anything, I will be there for you. Just call me". I thanked him once again and he left.

It was a few months after the accident before I went to see my husband again but he was good with that because he wanted me to get well. He had been calling four or five times a day so we were in communication but hell, my phone bill was high...very high.

It had been the beginning of June, around my birthday June 5th, when for the very first time after the accident I had went up to see my husband on a visit. It was such a good visit. I was able to kiss my man, hug him, and I even got a few feels of Big Daddy, it was great!!! I had not felt Big Daddy in a long time. We talked about what the plan was going to be and I said I was going to work out my budget for my Player's Ball this year. Antoine said, "Oh, I forgot your money making party", I said, "yes and I need to get the artists back in the studio". We talked about his business and what has happened when I was not able to come up and he said it was hurting (meaning his business), but his business did not matter if his wife was not well. I smiled and kissed him, I then mentioned to him about my visit from Mr. Biggs. Antoine first asked if Brandy came with him, I said "no, but she started a federal government job so she probably was at work", Antoine said, "ok", then he asked about the visit and what was he visiting me for. I told him that Brandy wanted to know if I was ok after the accident so she asked him to check up on me. Antoine said "ok, that was nice". We continue our visit and then it was time to leave. I kissed him and left.

It was now the following weekend after my birthday. I was getting ready to go to Brooklyn to spend time with my best friend Rosie when I doorbell rang. I went to my door and it was Mr. Biggs, I said "Mr. Biggs, what's up?" Mr. Biggs responded, "Happy Birthday". I said "thank you but it was last week". He said "I know. I know you were with your husband, so I decided to come this weekend to take you out". I look at Mr. Biggs, and then I said "What is going on with Brandy?" Mr. Biggs looked at me and said "we are not together; you hold a special place in my heart". I looked at him and said "I am married and I don't need no problems", I then said, "Both of you (meaning my husband and Mr. Biggs) have the same kind of business so there could be war". Mr. Biggs said "I understand". He left and I continued to get myself ready to go to Brooklyn. I went on to Brooklyn to see my best friend Rosie, never mentioning this to her because I know that in the past I had gotten her in the middle of some stuff with Antoine and myself; so I needed to handle this on my own.

As the weeks went by and I continue to work, take my artists to the studio and run my business; as well as Antoine's, it was now around July. It was the week for me to go see my husband. I scheduled my trip with the bus company because I did not want to drive. I called Prison Gap, the bus company, and reserved my trip for that coming Saturday. The rest of the week I would work and Friday night I would leave. It was now Tuesday, I was looking over my life and I was just admiring that I had done ten years with my husband and he had five years left. I could not believe that the time had gone by so fast. I would only have five more years left to be alone before my husband would be back in the flesh; in my presence.

The phone rang and it was my husband. I heard the operator and then my husband saying his name so I said "yes I will accept", Antoine said "hey there", I said "hey Poppy, how are you?" He said," I'm doing good" and went right into business. After our conversation about both my business and his we discussed what we would be doing on the visit. So, it was agreed that we would try to sneak some loving because we both were horny; we had to do what we had to do. We spoke a little more and then the phone hung up so I continued to fix my clothes for the week. The telephone rang again and I said "yes" and heard someone say "yes to what?" and I said "who is this?" The voice said "it's Mr. Biggs", I said "Hey there Mr. Biggs. How are you?" He said "I assume that you must have been talking to your husband" I said "yes, and I thought it was him again, but it was you. Mr. Biggs, what is going on in your life that you need some attention?" I only spoke to Mr. Biggs like that because we were friends and if there was anyone he would confide in, it would be me. Mr. Biggs replied and said "look, I want to get some of that Players Ball money. I know that your party make a lot of money, so could you use a partner?" I said "I have not even thought of that and I am a little short on funds because of my accident; but, you can be my partner, splitting every expense down the middle." Mr. Biggs said "cool that sound like a plan." I said "when I come back from my visit with my husband we will meet and sign a contract for the 70's Player Ball event." Mr. Biggs agreed and we both said good night.

The next morning was just like all the other Wednesday morning; work, come home, get myself prepared for the studio with my artists, and going Uptown and to Brooklyn to take care of Antoine's business. Thursday went the same and Friday came in with a bang! Friday I went to work, did my usual route, dumped the truck, drove my truck to the garage, parked and gave my supervisor the dump ticket. I went home to get myself prepared to see my husband; the man that give me the energy and strength to go on another day. That evening at 59th Street and Columbus circle as I waited on the bus, I tried to figure out a way to confront my husband about my new partnership with Mr. Biggs; what I wanted to do and how I going to pull this off. Antoine had already been kind of upset before when Mr. Biggs came to check up on me after the accident. As the bus arrived, I got on the bus, found my assigned seat and started to think of a plan. The bus arrived at Groveland Correctional and I got on the line to visit my husband. I went through the standard process and then got into the visiting room to wait on Antoine to come down. As I notice him coming, I was happy but very nervous, being that I was still trying to find a way to let Antoine know about my plans for the Players Ball this year.

Antoine walked over to kiss me. We decided to go get the food and drinks before sitting down, so we walked over to the vending machine and got our regular 6 buffalo wings, 4 French fries, 2 Pepsi sodas, 2 snicker bars, and 2 popcorns. Then, we went to get tickets for the pictures. As we walked back I said "Antoine, how would you feel if I told you that I have a partner for the Players Ball event that I do every year?" Antoine said "well with a partner there wouldn't be so much on you but your numbers would double". I said "good, I have a partner". Antoine said "ok, who is it?" I said "Mr. Biggs, he wants to invest in the party. I told him that when I come back from the visit we would talk". Antoine said "as long as it's all business, I am good; but remember that if he try you it will be a problem and your friend Brandy won't have a man. I am trusting that my wife will hold her own." I said "ok poppy, thanks for believing in me." We continue to talk about all the other businesses, played our usual card games, took our picture, and of course we felt up one another by the picture booth; because it was always crowded and the C.O (Correction Officer) could not see us doing the nasty. I always sat on Antoine's lap in pictures but that was just me sitting on Big Daddy; riding my husband. We went back to the table and before you know it, it was three o' clock and the visit was over. I kissed my husband and said "bye, see you in two weeks". Antoine said "don't forget what I said about Mr. Biggs"; I said "yeah yeah".

Chapter XXXVII

Mr. Biggs

It was the month of July and I had two full months to promote this "Players Ball" in order to be successful as usual. I got to Columbus Circle and I was very tired; but I did not drive. So I decide to call Mr. Biggs to see if he was in Brooklyn. Maybe he could take me home. So when I dialed the number Mr. Biggs answered and said "I don't see you". I said "Mr. Biggs are you talking to someone?" Mr. Biggs said "I am talking to you". I said "I am at Columbus Circle". He said "ok, I will be there in a minute". I said "Mr. Biggs, can you drive me home?" Mr. Biggs said "yes". I said "thanks". He said "no problem". As we drove to New Jersey we talked about all kinds of subjects; it was all about business and the future of success. We also talked about the strategy of how we would promote the party this year. As we got closer to the house Mr. Biggs said to me, "if you are ever in Staten Island and need to go to the bathroom, shower or take a nap"..... He then handed me his apartment key. I looked at Mr. Biggs and said "what do you think I would do with your house key?" Mr. Biggs said "if you need it, use it, because I am in Brooklyn. I don't stay on Staten Island anymore seeing that Brandy and I have not been together. You still do a lot of business in Staten Island so you may get tired and need a place". I said "thank you", got out of the car, and went into my house. Soon as I got into my house, I took my clothes off, jumped into the shower, and went to sleep.

The next two weeks were the same; working, promoting the Players Ball, and studio time with the artists; Ruff Rugged and Real, Janetta, and Samuel. We went to the radio station to meet with DJ Red alert and the host of the Players Ball, Bugsy. We also went to Bedford Avenue in Brooklyn to meet Ralph McDaniels at his store. After that we met with the Photographer, all the other acts and the Promoter. The following week we were purchasing stuff for the event; Whoops, Click Clacks, dice, etc. Mr. Biggs and I were really working hard for the Players Ball. We decide to stop early one evening, go eat out, and then Mr. Biggs took me to my car. It was always nice having someone drive you around. I had missed that with my husband. Mr. Biggs said "I will see you after your visit". I said "ok, see you next week". Mr. Biggs knew that this would be the weekend for my husband. It was Friday and I was putting all my stuff in the car. I was going to drive for the first time after my accident to see the man]; the man of my life, my husband, the man that I asked GOD for and because GOD loved me "He" gave Antoine to me.

As I drove to Groveland Correctional I was thinking that it was very short coming and that this journey will be over soon. It was less than five years that I had left to do this complete bid. I was just as excited driving to see him as I am with him. I get to the correctional facility and get on the line to wait through the process of: them calling your name, asking you questions, and checking your full body. After that, I walk over to the visitors waiting area to wait for my husband. As I see Antoine coming I get real excited because I've been missing him every day that I am with another man. Antoine said "Hey there Mrs. B", I say "hey there Mr. B". He said "How are things going?" I say "they are going well". He said "how is the new Partner?" I say "he is ok". Antoine asked, "How is the event and promotion going?" I said "they are going good. The financial part is completely done". Antoine asked, "Everyone is paid?" I said "yes, that's the good thing about having a partner; it's not all on me". Antoine said "HMMM...." I said "what does that mean?" Antoine said "nothing". Then we talked about the business and went to get our food and tickets for pictures. I really felt uncomfortable so I said" is there something you want to say or ask?" Antoine said "yes". I said shoot (meaning speak) He said, "I want to know if you sleeping with him". I said "NO". Antoine said "ok, I'll ask you again another time". I said "why?" He said, "There is too much time being spent amongst you two". I said "do you want me to stop?" Antoine said "I will leave it up to you". I kissed my husband and it was time to go. We never got to take the picture or get some loving because our conversation about Mr. Biggs was so intense. Time flew by. I left, got in my car, and drove back home. It was about 10:00pm when I got to my house.

July 1999 had come in and there was one month left to promote with my partner. This event had to be promoted hard, leaving nothing on the table; so I went running with my boots on the ground and so did Mr. Biggs; he promoted as well. We were in different cities and boroughs all the time but Mr. Biggs asked me to meet him in Staten Island for a meeting to discuss the party. I went to the diner where he asked me to meet him but he did not show up. So I went to the apartment. I used my key and I opened the door but it was empty so I called his name out loud; no response. After walking in further, I noticed dinner was cooked and my Moet was on the table. I called again "Mr. Biggs?" and there was no answer. I fixed my food, poured a glass of champagne, turned the TV on and then I noticed a note on the dresser; it was address to me. It said "hey I will not be coming back. I had an emergency in Brooklyn. I am sorry. Hope you enjoy". It was so late; about 12:00 am by the time I finished eating, drinking and watching TV so I decided to stay. I took a shower and got into bed.

It was about 4:00 am when I felt someone get in the bed; it was not a dream. It was Mr. Biggs; kissing on my neck, then he was on my breast, then he went down to my belly, then he ate me like a hungry man eats his lunch. Before I could say anything, Mr. Biggs was inside of me and it felt so good. I had not been touched and eaten like that since my trailer visits. I could not believe how I responded to another man and it felt right. We made love all morning and afternoon. I was open to another man; a man that was in my presence and not behind bars. What was I going to say to my husband? I was open to making love with another man; Mr. Biggs knew all of what I had been missing. Mr. Biggs was my secret!!! Mr. Biggs kissed me like my husband kissed me and he touched me the same as Antoine. He was the same kind of man; Gentle, Kind, Lovable. What was I going to do? Mr. Biggs was my man at home; my husband was in prison.

Business scheduling:
Rafaela can be reach at via email for;

Public book signing:
Themanyhatsofawomen@gmail.com.

Private booking signing:
Themanyhatsofawomen@gmail.com

Public speaking events at:
Themanyhatsofawomen@gmail.com

Inspiration & motivation venues:
themanyhatsofawomen@gmail.com

CPSIA information can be obtained
at www.ICGtesting.com
Printed in the USA
BVHW071523090919
557952BV00001B/183/P